**DATE DUE**

| 860430 | | | |
|---|---|---|---|
| SEP 2 1986 | | OCT 0 2 1991 | |
| DEC 2 1 1987 | | MAY 19 1994 | |
| | | | |
| SEP 29 1988 | | MAR 1 4 1995 | |
| | | SEP 1 4 1995 | |
| | | | |
| MAY 2 2 | | | |
| | | | |
| MAR 1 3 1991 | | | |
| | | | |
| NOV 1 9 1991 | | | |
| JAN 0 4 1993 | | | |
| | | | |
| | | | |
| | | | |
| | | | |
| | | | |
| | | | |

# THE COUNSELOR'S
# DESK MANUAL

# THE COUNSELOR'S DESK MANUAL

## A CLINICAL HANDBOOK

*By*

### KENNETH URIAL GUTSCH

*Director of Training*
*Department of Counseling Psychology*
*University of Southern Mississippi*
*Hattiesburg, Mississippi*

### JACK LEMORE DANIELS

*Director of the Counseling Laboratory*
*Department of Counseling Psychology*
*University of Southern Mississippi*
*Hattiesburg, Mississippi*

*With a Foreword by*

**William Joseph Weikel**

*Past President*
*American Mental Health Counselor's Association*
*Professor of Education*
*Morehead State University*
*Morehead, Kentucky*

CHARLES C THOMAS • PUBLISHER
*Springfield • Illinois • U.S.A.*

*Published and Distributed Throughout the World by*

CHARLES C THOMAS • PUBLISHER

2600 South First Street

Springfield, Illinois 62717

*1-217-789-8980*

*With* THOMAS BOOKS *careful attention is given to all details of manufacturing and
design. It is the Publisher's desire to present books that are satisfactory as to their physical
qualities and artistic possibilities and appropriate for their particular use.* THOMAS
BOOKS *will be true to those laws of quality that assure a good name and good will.*

*Printed in the United States of America*
*Q-R-3*

*Library of Congress Cataloging in Publication Data*

Gutsch, Kenneth Urial.
    The counselor's desk manual.

    Bibliography: p.
    Includes index.
    1. Counseling--Handbooks, manuals, etc.   I. Daniels,
Jack Lemore. II. Title. [DNLM: 1. Counseling--
handbooks.   WM 34 G984c]
    BF637.C6G873 1985              158'.3              84-26810
    ISBN 0-398-05114-3

# FOREWORD

OVER the past twenty-five years, counseling has evolved from a service or "specialty" requiring minimal graduate training, to a complex and dynamic discipline with an extensive body of knowledge. Training that was once provided through part-time or summer institutes is now deemed inadequate and has been replaced by comprehensive graduate programs with extensive clinical and practicum experience.

The beginning counselors of today may find themselves working in a variety of settings, some unheard of even a few years ago. In addition to being involved in traditional settings such as public school settings, college settings, rehabilitation settings, and mental health agencies, increasing numbers of counselors and psychotherapists will find employment in hospitals, private counseling agencies, hospices, industrial settings and private businesses. Many counselors will decide to offer their services in the private sector through full or part-time practices or by joining with other health care professionals to develop HMO's, PPO's or EAP's. Most counselors will find that they must be conversant with physicians, nurses and other health care providers, as well as with other core professionals in psychiatry, psychology, clinical social work and psychiatric nursing.

The *Counselor's Desk Manual: A Clinical Handbook* is the first book that I have seen that is written for today's new breed of professional counselors. Within these pages are provided the techniques, theories and practical information crucial to the counselor's expanding role. As a counselor-educator I welcome this book as a much needed addition to a field glutted with texts covering only narrow aspects of the discipline. As a practioner I will reserve a space on my desk for this practical book, because it promises to be a reference destined for frequent use in the coming years.

Bill Weikel, Ph.D.
Past President, A.M.H.C.A.
Professor of Education
Morehead State University
Morehead, Kentucky

# PREFACE

PERHAPS the one thing we can say about counselors today is that they are better trained than ever before. Those who graduate from nationally accredited training programs reflect an excellent image of professionalism. However, the profession of counseling is no different from any other profession. It needs structure. No profession has identity except through the process by which it is implemented. Counseling is simply a vehicle language through which behavior change becomes possible. The skills of the professional counselor, however, cannot be enforced until they are couched within the legal, ethical, and moral contingencies by which, and through which, counseling finds its functional identity.

We have a friend who is fond of the saying: "If the only tool you have is a hammer, you'll treat everything like a nail." To save counselors from the fate of treating all their clients (patients) in the same way, we have developed a resource manual which covers a breadth of experiences. By so doing, we have introduced them to a diversity of subjects which go beyond basic relationship skills and touch on such areas as how to contract with clients, when to contract with clients, what purpose the contract serves, how to deal with ethical issues, how to determine if a client is using drugs or alcohol excessively, how to correspond with others on behalf of one's client, how to help one's client deal with stress, how to handle potential suicide cases, and how to help one's client deal with anxiety.

Basically, we have approached the subject of counseling from this perspective because it seems obvious that our professional world of counseling teeters between an understanding of theories on the one hand and the development of an ambience by which those theories can be practiced, on the other. In essence, our efforts have been to provide resource information for counselors (i.e., school counselors, community mental health counselors, private practitioners, marriage and family counselors, crises interventionists, social workers, school psychologists, and drug-alcohol counselors). Then too, *The Counselor's Desk Manual* is an excellent resource book for clinical and counselor training programs. It is, as a matter of fact, one of the sources which we have developed for training counseling pschologists at the University of Southern Mississippi. In this respect, we hope it serves you as well as it serves us.

# ACKNOWLEDGMENTS

THE COUNSELOR'S DESK MANUAL is the product of many years of work as counselor-educators and counseling psychologists. The concepts and procedures all grew out of the day-to-day training experiences of the authors and have been carefully blended into a manual for the convenience of those who want to take advantage of this knowledge. Ideas, suggestions, and criticisms have been offered by countless students and colleagues. In this particular case, we want to thank:

Doug McMillan, John Magee, Robert Powell, Mark Barron, Steve Lo Bello and Susan Sheridan for their vigilance in bringing new materials to our attention;

Kim Faulkner for his help in preparing the section on substance abuse;

Laura Lee Rockwell, University of Iowa; Janie Rugg, Jackson Public Schools; Genevieve Burris, Pascagoula Public Schools and Jeannie Koestler, Vicksburg Community Mental Health Center for their willingness to read and critique this manuscript;

Paula Sanford and Betty Lane for typing and organizing the manuscript;

John D. Alcorn for his adminstrative support as chairman of the Department of Counseling Psychology.

# CONTENTS

## Section II — Procedures and Treatment Protocols

## Section III — Forms, Contracts and Letters

## Section IV — Ethics and Issues

# THE COUNSELOR'S
# DESK MANUAL

## SECTION I

# COUNSELING: THE APPLICATION OF PSYCHOLOGICAL PRINCIPLES

THIS section is written to assist the counselor in developing an overview of the direction in which we feel the profession is heading. Section I is an introduction to counseling; it includes a sketch of impressions of the different models used in counseling and of the techniques through which counseling models become manifest.

# AN INTRODUCTION TO COUNSELING

COUNSELING, like psychotherapy, has been defined and redefined many times. The reason for this seems obvious. Before one can train a person to do something so abstruse as counseling, one must first establish a baseline understanding of the concept in question. To establish such an understanding may be to recognize counseling as a process. By so doing, it becomes possible to define in terms of the psychological principles and techniques involved in that process.

To expand on this would be to say that counseling involves the implementation of those psychological principles and techniques which help the recipient (the client) to reorganize cognitively and to act behaviorally in ways which result in greater personal satisfaction and effectiveness. If this is true, at least to the extent to which we believe it to be true, then the essence of counseling as a process lies in the principles and techniques through which it is implemented. What this really means is that the potential for effective counseling increases when the counselor understands how to apply those psychological principles essential to change. For example, a male student may request counseling services to gain information about dating. The counselor, if he or she is to help this student, must understand the psychological principles of relating, i.e. those principles which emerge as laws founded on psychological research. It now appears that without such an understanding, there can be no uniform methods of intervention, no conceptualizations of direction, no foundation from which to start therapy, no psychological laws upon which to rely for treatment, and therefore, no science or corpus of knowledge upon which to make judgements about behavior change (Kluckhohn and Murray, 1969).

Basically, one might say that the essence of counseling rests with the proper application of well researched scientific principles. Ultimately these principles can become manifest through theoretical models. A model might include such principles as nearness, similarity and reward; nearness meaning that you have to be in contact with someone if you want to get to know that person, similarity implying that you must have something in common with the other person if the relationship is to experience cohesiveness, and reward meaning that you must feel good about being in the relationship as it continues to grow. Contingencies which affect these principles might include one's awareness of these principles and how to use them in order to change a relationship. Let's extend this concept for a moment and say that we have a young man who has never before dated and that he introduces as his presenting problem the idea, "I'm not sure how to ask a girl for a date." Say, for the sake of illustrative purposes, that we refer to this young man as Bob and that as he expands on his feelings of apprehension about girls he also includes his concerns about meeting girls, talking with girls and asking girls for dates. This is, in part, a problem involving the application of information to effect better girl-boy relationships. What Bob needs is to develop a dating strategy in which he understands and utilizes the principles of nearness, similarity and reward. If his counselor knows how to supply this information, then perhaps he or she can help Bob. Once Bob understands how to use these principles, the counselor may encourage Bob's participation in a personal growth group composed of both males and females who are interested in learning more about dating. Within such a setting Bob could become involved in such techniques as role playing, role reversal and/or role observation which, through direct feedback from his female counterparts, might give him some ideas about what kind of a person he appears to be, how girls like to be approached when someone is asking for a date, and how well he is performing in terms of his stated objective — preparing to ask for a date. The entire group might also participate in reflecting on his general appearance, his personality as they see it, and his fluency. In addition, the counselor and the other group members may set up a training sequence to help Bob prepare a *backup system* ( a system of alternative directions Bob can take), should his plans for relating go amiss. A successful *backup system* provides a person with recourse. Thus, in Bob's case, we have a person who will be less likely to fail because he has developed backup alternatives. This safeguard to failure makes behavior change more appealing since it increases the potential for success. What Bob is really learning in his search for information about dating is how to function as an autonomous individual and how to gain closeness to people. He has gone to a counselor and the counselor has elicited the help of a personal growth group to make Bob aware of a process by which he can function more effectively.

Once Bob has the necessary information about dating and has tested this information against reality through role playing experiences, he must then generalize from his personal growth group experiences to an *in vivo* experience. That is, once Bob has developed an awareness of how he relates to women within his growth group, his next step is to make some decision about whom to ask for a date, when to ask for a date and under what circumstances to ask for a date.

Naturally his counselor and members of the group are in a position to give him some hints about how to monitor the progress of a potential relationship before asking for a date. These hints will help him to know whether or not the girl he is thinking about asking for a date is reflecting positive-dating-cues. At this point, Bob should be thinking about applying the information he has gained to the transition from where he is to where he wants to go. This transition will probably take place gradually and might involve the following sequence of steps:

(a) Since Bob has gained some understanding about himself and his potential for functioning within a dating relationship, he may now want to risk generalizing from a safe situation with his counselor and group members to a real life situation in which what he has learned is put to the acid test.

(b) If his *backup* system helps him to feel confident about himself and in control of his life, Bob may then risk asking a girl for a date.

(c) If successful, he should experience positive reinforcement and his interests in dating should increase.

(d) If unsuccessful, his *backup* system should temper the impact of rejection. That is, because he has a backup system, he still has alternatives which he can attempt as he makes corrections in his approach to dating. Planning his backup system with his counselor should have helped him to understand that pitfalls are a normal part of risking and that risking is the essence of behavior change.

From this illustration, it should be clear that a counselor is an agent of change who combines psychological principles with personal observations in an effort to effect such change. To maintain structure the counselor works from a theoretical model; the model is reaffirmed through specific techniques and the techniques are supported by research. Thus, to be an effective counselor, it seems that one must have a theorectical model from which to work; the theory must become manifest through the specific techniques which are applied within a contingency of relating; and the techniques must emerge from psychological principles established through research.

Basically, psychological research has been responsible for establishing at least four well defined theorectical models from which counselors draw *in total* or *eclectically*: Intrapsychic, Behavioral, Phenomenological, and Cognitive-Behavioral.

## A. Model I — Intrapsychic Theory (Dynamic Psychology)

A counselor using this model in its purest form or drawing from it *eclectically* contends that problems such as those involving incorrect information, incorrect inferences, the inability to distinguish between imagination and reality (Beck, 1976) or the inability to make responsible decisions are an extension of insidious operations of past events. The primary impetus of the counselor would be to discover *why* people act as they do. The essence of this model is the belief that with the advent of childhood anxiety, there is a progressive, sequential development of defensive maneuvers designed to combat anxiety. In practice these two determinants of behavior, i.e. (a) *childhood anxiety,* and (b) the *defensive strategies implemented to combat this anxiety*, are unconscious. Therefore, it is the unique purpose of the counselor using this model to discover the repressed and elusive phenomena which cause anxiety and the specific defense maneuvers incorporated by the person to prevent a resurgence of anxiety (Gutsch, Sisemore, & Williams, 1984, p.4).

## Techniques

The techniques employed by a counselor using this model as a basis from which to work might include, but would not necessarily be restricted to:

(a) Dream Interpretation
(b) Free Association
(c) Word Association
(d) Projective Testing
(e) Personal Sharing (catharsis)
(f) Regression (taking the person back in time to an earlier period)
(g) Observation (systematic)
(h) Confrontation
(i) Relationship Analysis
(j) Relaxation

All techniques related to this model are, or should be, designed to deal with the unconscious. The idea is that the person does not know that the influencing stimulus (the instinct), which arises from within the organism itself, is repressed. Therefore, the counselor must use techniques which both define the repressed material and reveal the impact it has on the person.

## B. Model II — Behavior Theory

A second model to which a counselor might subscribe is known as behavior theory. It is the contention of behaviorists that ineffective and indecisive behavior is learned, and that it develops according to the same laws as those governing effective and decisive behavior. They further contend that reinforcers shape behavior and that differences in behavior result from differential reinforcement of successive approximations (Gutsch, Sisemore, & Williams, 1984, p. 107).

## Techniques

The techniques which are employed by a counselor using this model would include, but would not necessarily be limited to:

(a) Counter Conditioning (direct conditioning)
(b) Modeling (social imitation or demonstration)
(c) Shaping (using positive reinforcers such as tokens)
(d) Prompting and Fading
(e) Response Differentiation
(f) Punishment
(g) Verbal Appeal
(h) Flooding
(i) Negative Adaptation (changing fear by repeated exposure to fear)
(j) Disuse
(k) Premack

The effectiveness of these techniques is based on how behavior is changed and how the change is reinforced. Reinforcers are motivators (sometimes considered rewards) for completing tasks. For example, in a counseling situation, Skinner (1953) would probably suggest the following four schedules for reinforcement:

(a) **Fixed Ratio Schedule** — Fixed ratio means that there are a fixed number of responses which must be made before a reinforcer (a reward) is forthcoming. In a fixed ratio 5 (FR5) schedule a reinforcer is applied for every 5th response. For example, in the garment industry an FR5 might mean that for every 5 blouses completed by a seamstress, she would receive one dollar (a reinforcer). The faster she worked, the more money she would make. Another example might involve getting a client to complete $x$ number of task orientations; that is, assuming that the client is capable, a counselor might set up a training paradigm which will reinforce the client positively for each task completed. If the reinforcer is something the client really wants, then the consistency with which the client works will determine the amount of reinforcement achieve. Suppose that the counselor uses "uh huh" as a positive reinforcer (a motivator which tells the client that he or she is on target). Suppose also that the more the client talks about those things which are significant to counseling the more "uh huhs" are given as responses. The counselor might, at first, use "uh huh" to reinforce *each significant contribution* (FR1). Ultimately the counselor might reinforce every fifth contributions of significance (FR5). As a result, the client would increase the rate at which significant contributions were made in an effort to achieve positive reinforcement as soon as possible.

(b) **Fixed Interval Schedule** — An example of a fixed interval schedule would be to have a counselor contract for a positive reinforcer on the basis of a completed performance. If the client completed his or her assignments when the due date arrived, he or she would then be given a positive reinforcer (a reward). The problem with the FI schedule is that clients seldom make any effort to complete the schedule until the due date. At best, that could create a marginal product.

(c) **Variable Ratio Reinforcement** — Variable ratio reinforcement is just what the phrase implies, i.e. reinforcement which varies with trials. For example, if a counselor reinforced only quality performance on tasks for which his or her client contracted, the client, who was unaware of which tasks were to be positively reinforced, would have to do his or her best on each task in order to receive the reinforcer. This is a strong schedule. If the client really wants the positive reinforcer, not knowing which of his or her tasks is to be considered quality performance will keep the client working at peak levels all the time. Say for example that a counselor had a male client who wanted to date girls and had reached a point where he was ready to risk asking for a date. Variable ratio reinforcement would take place if on the first two attempts at dating the client was rejected and then finally on his third attempt, he got a date (positive reinforcement). Variable reinforcement in this case would help the client to understand that dating is a process at which he can be successful if he practices the rules by which it takes place.

(d) **Variable Interval Schedule** — You may have noticed that whereas ratio reinforcement schedules deal with trials (attempts) to accomplishment, interval schedules deal with time. The variable interval schedule means that reinforcement occurs on an average of so many times per hour, per day, per week or per month. Perhaps this schedule is analogous to variable scheduling in terms of the length of the counseling session. One example of how this might occur exists when a counselor refuses to work a full fifty minutes with the client unless the client remains on task. Thus, the client, if he or she is to be reinforced, must constantly remain on task. In this case, task preparation is perpetual, and the client learns effective task orientation at a slow but steady pace.

Another example of how this schedule works would be to assume that the counselor is working with a young couple who has just entered into an argument. Both parties request conjoint counseling services but the counselor decides that the only time he or she will see them conjointly is if both of them work at a peak of therapeutic performance during concurrent counseling sessions. When that occurs, the counselor agrees to do conjoint counseling. The situation now exists as one in which both clients move along slowly but at a consistently high performance level so that each can be reinforced by the presence of the other in conjoint therapy.

## Model III — Phenomenological Theory
### (Self-Theory)

It is the contention of phenomenological theorists that the distinctiveness of one's conscious experience — one's inner reality, should be the primary concern of the counselor or facilitator. In essence, phenomenologists believe that the focus of intepersonal relations should be on what is real to the acting individual and not necessarily on what is physically observable to the counselor. Thus, the essence of counseling, according to this model, should involve an awareness on the part of the client, i.e. the essence of counseling is a figure-ground shift which makes the client aware of another point of view. Another way of putting this might be to say that the client would be encouraged to understand his or her inner reality from having participated in it, having become conscious of it, and having related to it. This experience helps the person to come into contact with a "new" and "different" reality which was not present before counseling was initiated. In this respect, it might be said that the phenomenological counselor will get each client to participate in, become conscious of and relate to both sides of an issue before making a decision about the issue (Gutsch, Sisemore, & Williams, 1984, p. 187).

*Techniques*

The techniques employed by a phenomenological counselor using this model would include but would not necessarily be restricted to the following self-awareness and/or self-concept enhancing exercises which can create a figure-ground shift:

(a) Role Playing
(b) Role Reversal
(c) Role Substitution
(d) The Open chair
(e) Relationship Analysis
(f) Dream Interpretation
(g) Free Association
(h) Personal Sharing (self disclosure)
(i) Leveling
(j) Breaking Out (with groups)
(k) Breaking In (with groups)
(l) Feedback Experiences
(m) Touching Experiences
(n) Inner Circle — Outer Circle Experiences (with groups)

## D. Model IV — Cognitive-Behavior Theory

It is the contention of cognitive-behavior counselors that misunderstandings in life result from faulty beliefs and/or thoughts which create ineffective response patterns. They believe that the thought process can be contaminated by arbitrary inferences, overgeneralizations and grossly magnified distortions. In essence, they attempt to help people establish a reality base from which they can work. They also believe that people typically are capable of thinking their way into a new way of acting or acting their way into a new way of thinking. As a result, their approach to counseling places a great deal of emphasis on "*What*" a person is doing and not on "*Why*" he or she is doing it (Gutsch, Sisemore, & Williams, 1984, p. 221).

*Techniques*

The techniques employed in cognitive-behavior theory vary from counselor to counselor with such prominent theorists as Meichenbaum (1977) using *Stress Inoculation Training*; Mahoney (1977) using the *Personal Science Model*; Beck (1976) using *Cognitive Rehearsal*; Gutsch and Ritenour (1978) using *Cognitive and Behavioral Framing and Re-Framing*; and Ellis (1973) using a Rational-Emotive Approach, i.e. a sequence of steps including but not restricted to:

(a) Forcing clients to look at what they are saying.
(b) Teaching clients how to respond differently.

(c) Giving clients homework assignments.

(d) Helping clients to understand that to change their behavior, they must challenge their belief system.

These techniques, if properly implemented, are designed to create a climate in which self-assessment, self-observation, self-direction, self-acceptance, scientific thinking, flexibility, tolerance, commitment and risk become the rule rather than the exception. This model differs from the others most vividly in that it encourages process orientation, i.e. the ability to evaluate oneself, not on the basis of what one thinks but rather on the effectiveness of the process used in thinking. This model leans toward efficacy, but does not necessarily mandate that the objectives defined will become the goals attained. Rather, through the model, the person will learn that goal orientation is a gradual *process* and that failure is imminent *only* when he or she stops working toward such goals. Feeling good about yourself has to do with knowing that you have the best possible process for reaching your goals.

## SYNTHESIS

All of these models have certain common elements. That is, they all operate to perform a function; they all have structure or operational baselines from which they emerge, and they are all governed by well researched psychological principles which are significant in explaining how people relate. For example, a counselor may ask such questions as:

A.  How do people get their impressions of others?

B.  How do people influence others?

C.  How do people change their attitudes?

D.  How are people motivated?

Let's start answering these questions by going to research studies which address these issues directly.

A.  In an effort to answer the question, **"How do people get their impressions of others?"**, we can look at the following research studies:

1.  *Primacy Effect*
    **Research**: Asch, S.E., 1946
    **Principle**: The order in which you present information influences the person receiving the information. For example, a person described as *"envious — stubborn — critical — industrious and intelligent,"* is rated less favorably by another person than is a person who is described as *"intelligent — industrious — critical — stubborn and envious."* Second, changing an adjective can change an impression. That is, a person described as "intelligent — skillful — industrious — *warm* — determined — practical and cautious," is viewed differently from a person who is described as "intelli-

gent — skillful — industrious — *cold* — determined — practical and cautious." In this case, the terms "warm" and "cold" are referred to as Central Traits because they are central in influencing one person's impressions of another (Wishner, 1960).

**Importance of Counseling**: (a) Both what a counselor says and the way he or she says it are important in relating; (b) since some people are extremely guarded about relating with others, it is quite possible that in such relationships, much of what people say is clothed in a *metalanguage*. For example, just as in the primacy effect, the first words one hears are important, so in a conversation, the first statements to which a counselor is exposed become important. In counseling, as in life, those statements may be used as a MASK to create an impression. When this happens, it prevents the counselor from understanding the true feelings of the client.

2. *Physical Attractiveness*

**Research**: Walster, E., Aronson, V., Abrahams, D., & Rottman, L., 1966; Dion, K., 1972; Sigall, H., & Landy, D., 1973.

**Principle**: People who are physically attractive are perceived more positively than those who are physically unattractive.

**Importance to Counseling**: Some years ago the authors were doing research in one of the public elementary schools when the principal said, "I'll bet I can pick out the students who will be referred to my office today." As the students came into the school building, he proceeded to point out those children he thought would be referred to his office. Since the project base was in an adjoining office, it was easy to check on his accuracy. Interestingly enough, at the end of the day it was found that he was extremely accurate. He was asked whether or not he knew who would be referred because the same children were referred each day. He said, "In part that's true. However, I know by watching to see how they're dressed and how clean they are. If they're dirty, they'll be referred almost immediately . . . if they're only poorly dressed, then chances are a bit slimmer."

Counselors are probably as biased as anyone else. Therefore personal attractiveness will probably play as important a role in what a counselor does for a student or client as what the student or client does in order to maintain the relationship with the counselor. Thus, physical attractiveness plays an important role in how well the client relates to others outside the counseling setting. To be accepted, physical attractiveness is important.

3. *Nearness*

**Research**: Byrne, D., 1971

**Principle**: We like people who share our attitudes and interests. We also like people who live near us or work in close proximity with us.

**Importance to Counseling**: If a counselor is to change the behavior of a client, the counselor must maintain a relationship (nearness) with that person. It is *not* necessary for counselors to agree with everything someone else says. It is however, extremely important for people to understand that counselors are capable of working effectively with people who hold points of view which are not always supported by the consensus of society. The counselor, as a master of the figure-ground shift, must be ready to view both sides of an issue. If clients are to change their relationships with others, it is important for them to learn this principle and how to enforce it.

4. *Needs Complementarity*
**Research**: Daniel, W. J., 1943; Sherif & Sherif, 1956
**Principle**: While similarity attracts people, there must be some reward to maintain the relationship. That reward is sometimes found as two or more people or groups work together to accomplish an objective that could not be accomplished by one person alone. The idea of superordinate goals is a perfect illustration of this principle.
**Importance to Counseling**: The importance of this psychological principle is particularly obvious in the Sherif & Sherif (1956) study in which 22 boys who just arrived at a camp were randomly assigned to one of two groups, i.e. the Rattlers and the Eagles. The boys were approximately eleven years of age and before arriving at camp did not know each other, nor that they were about to become part of an experiment in conflict resolution.

Conflict was created between the two groups by having them compete. The conflict was exacerbated by frustrating one group and making the other group appear responsible. Utlimately what happended was that each group tried to be rougher, tougher and nastier than the other. At one point, the Eagles burned the Rattlers' flag and the Rattlers retaliated with bunkhouse raids, name calling and fist fighting.

To reduce the hositility between the two groups, the leaders brought them into close contact through play activities and eating, but the groups refused to intermingle. Other approaches were used, i.e. such things as verbal appeal, but without success. Finally they were brought together almost by accident when on an overnight trip, a truck which was used to transport their food "stalled" and the boys used a rope (which they normally used for a tug-of-war) to pull the vehicle to camp. At first, when the vehicle stalled, they looped the rope through the bumper and the two groups pulled on different ends. However, when the truck stalled again the next day, both groups intermingled as they pulled on the two ends and thus obliterated their group divisions. Since one group could not do the job alone, both groups worked together to accomplish the task. At the close of the experiment, Rattlers' choices of Eagles as friends went up from 6.4 to 36.4 percent, while Eagles' choices of Rattlers as friends increased from 7.5 to 23.2 percent.

5. *Cost/Benefit Ratio*

**Research**: Thibaut, J. W., & Kelley, H. H., 1959.

**Principle**: We like those people who reward us in some way. Thibaut and Kelley (1959) suggest that people look at the cost/benefit ratio involved in their respective relationships and pursue those relationships with the lowest personal cost and the greatest personal benefit.

**Importance to Counseling**: Counselors are in a position where relating is the essence of their effectiveness. They literally have to create cohesive (trusting) relationships almost on contact. Yet, the relationships that people enter into with counselors are really governed by such variables as cost/benefit ratios. What that means is that the relationship itself has to be worth something or it simply will not exist. Since people who seek counseling seldom experience intolerable pain, it would seem that learning how to relate well is vital to the counselor's effectiveness. Thus one might say, "Counselors have their work cut out for them." One of the few things a counselor can do for a client on initial contact is to listen to what that client has to say. Over the years, it has become increasingly obvious that many counselors do not listen carefully, that presenting problems and real problems are almost always different and that what people need most is accurate information — while what they need least is advice. Now, with the understanding of cost/benefit ratio, the counselor can comprehend the need for creating a climate which encourages the client to return.

B. To answer the question, **"How do people influence others?"** here are some of the studies and principles which are important:

1. *Conformity*

**Research**: Sherif, M., 1937

**Principle**: The idea is that people conform to group norms. How this is done can be seen in a study by Sherif (1937) in which he used autokinetic phenomenon (an illusion which causes a person in a dark room to believe that a dot of light, which is actually stationary, appears to be moving); Sherif found that when subjects were asked how far the light moved, judgments made by individuals varied widely. However, when subjects were in groups, they reached a consensus of opinion rather rapidly. This seems to indicate that when individuals are faced with ambiguous situations, they are influenced by the opinions of others.

Eysenck (1959) would, of course, point out that consistent conformity can lead to a dysthemic personality disorder. Schacter (1951), on the other hand, would say that the impact of conformity would depend on whether or not the person was *a deviant* (one who did not conform to group norms but had the satisfaction of maintaining his or her own personality); *a slider* (one who first showed opposition to the group's position but later revised his or her position); or a *no mode* (a person who showed no opposition to the group and always adopted the position of the group).

**Importance to Counseling**: Understanding the principle of conformity helps the counselor to decipher the metalanguage of the client. It helps the counselor to recognize factors other than those about which the client is talking as significant in shaping the client's life. For example, when the client says, "I don't want to go to college," is he or she saying that this is my decision or that it is a decision with which I must live if I want to remain a member of a group which is not college bound. Recognizing the client's metalanguage, the counselor can use an intervention strategy based on a broader perspective. That is, the counselor can now assume hypotheses which are broader than the stated problems. In this case the counselor can say, "Is that a peer group commitment?" By checking hypotheses this way the counselor can sometimes expedite his or her understanding of the case and how best to work with the client. The client, on the other hand, learns that he or she does not need to use handicapping strategies* with the counselor.

2. *Compliance*

**Research**: Homans, G. C., 1961

**Principle**: A person who feels quilty about how he or she has been treating someone else is more likely to comply with that person's requests. In essence, compliance is an outgrowth of exchange theory, i.e. the idea that how one operates depends on how rewards are allocated in proportion to investments.

One example of getting people to comply with a large favor involves getting them to comply with a small favor first and later, after you have a "*foot-in-the-door*," request a large favor. This is not totally unlike Festinger's (1957) dissonance theory.

Another technique sometimes referred to as the "*door-in-the-face*" technique, is used to gain small favors by asking for extreme favors first (requests that will probably be turned down), and then making smaller, more moderate requests. The idea is based on the concept of quilt and recognizes that people are more likely to comply with a sensible and more moderate request when they have turned down a large one.

A third technique involves judgment and conformity. Some years ago

---

*Handicapping strategies are strategies that prevent a person from achieving his or her real potentials in life. They are used by people because they serve a purpose. In many cases they protect the person from anticipated rejection.

Asch (1951) did a study in which subjects were asked to pick which of three (3) lines were equal in length to a standard line previously presented. *Although the correct answer was obvious*, confederates who were placed in the group to influence the answers of subjects, consistently gave incorrect answers. Ultimately the confederates actually influenced incorrect answers on ⅓ of the trials.

**Importance to Counseling**: Compliance is an important principle to counseling because it tells the counselor whether or not a client might change his or her behavior. The past frequently dictates what will happen in the future. By learning as much as possible about the client, the counselor will understand in what ways and under what conditions the client will repeat or deviate from his normal pattern of living. Knowing this, the counselor will understand how best to get the client to work on his or her deficiencies, i.e. incorrect understandings, incorrect inferences and inaccurate information.

3. *Obedience*

**Research**: Hofling, C., et al., 1966; Milgram, S., 1974

**Principle**: People submit to those in authoritative roles. One example of obedience which is quite interesting emerges in Hofling's *et al.* (1966) study of the power of roles. In his study, a nurse conforms to a psychiatrist's demands by giving the patient 20 mg. of Astroten instead of the 5 mg. mandated by prescription. The results of the study seem to indicate that a nurse, because of her position or "pecking order," will sometimes obey a doctor's orders even if the orders appear in conflict with her own knowledge and judgment. It may be that nurses assume this subordinate position because they are trained to this set.

The second example of obedience, which is both situational and dynamic, was introduced by Milgram (1974). In this particular research study, Milgram instructed one subject to serve as a "teacher," and a second subject (who was actually a confederate*) to serve as a learner. According to his instructions, it was the "teacher's" responsibility to get the learner (the confederate) to recall a series of words. To accomplish this objective, the "teacher" had to make a decision about administering high intensity shocks which were marked "DANGEROUS." In addition, the learner (the confederate) initially reported a heart condition (a condition which did not lend itself well to high intensity electrical shock). As you can readily see, the idea was to determine how many *"teachers"* would obey orders to shock their respective *"learners"* when they continued to make mistakes and how far they (the teachers) would go in terms of the intensity of shock they would apply to their respective learners.

---

*A confederate is a person who only pretends to be a research subject but is actually working with the researchers.

Results of this study indicated that 60 percent of Milgram's subjects (those designated as teachers) went all the way even though the learners (the confederates) cried out in pain and demanded that the *"teachers"* stop. It should be noted that this percentage was obtained when the experimenter was in the same room with the "teacher." When the experimenter left the room, however, the "teacher" became less obedient. This was also true when the "teacher" and "learner" (confederate) were not separated by rooms. Also noteworthy is the fact that when several "teachers" were in the same room together, obedience was determined by the influence of the group on each respective member of the group. Subjects (teachers) who refused to obey "all-the-way" were more likely to be less authoritative, more introspective and more tolerant of ambiguous situations.

**Importance to Counseling**: This research on obedience helps counselors to understand better why in family therapy or marriage and family counseling, certain members of the family (especially children) respond to authority figures in certain ways. Response patterns within a family are established over a long period of time. Therefore, when working with youngsters, counselors must remember that much of what a youngster does may be a reaction to the authority figures in his or her family rather than a proaction to his or her own goals. In a sense, the problems of a child are frequently part of an interlocking psychopathology within the family. That does not imply that every student who is indecisive about, and/or ineffective in, his or her life situations should have family therapy. All it means is that the value base from which the child emerges might have strong family roots. That could mean a strong attempt to be obedient and in conformity, or it could mean a strong effort to break loose and find one's own personal identity outside of the family.

Parents should remember that one result of their extensive use of authority (compliance) can be frustration. In the *Romeo and Juliet Effect*, for example, parental interference with the relationship intensified the love between Romeo and Juliet and forced them to choose between their love for their parents and their love for each other. The final choice was obvious (Driscoll, Davis, & Lipetz, 1972).

4. *Social Power*

**Research**: Hovland, C. I., Lumsdaine, A., & Sheffield, F., 1949; Hovland, C. I., 1957.

**Principle**: A person who is an expert, i.e. a person who is thought to have expertise because of such things as his or her college degree(s), has some authority over others. Another way of saying this would be to say that a person who is chosen as a model by others or who serves as a model by mandate, has referent power over others. One example of this can be seen in the Hofling et al. (1966) research where the psychiatrist prescribed 20 mg. of a drug (Astroten), more than was safely recommended, i.e. the normal dosage was listed on the pill box as 5 mg.; maximum dosage 10 mg. The psychiatrist had legitimate power over nurses not only because of his training as a medical doctor, but also because of their training as nurses.

**Importance to Counseling**: This idea also leads to a second principle which is complementary to the first, and that is the higher the credibility of those who voice their opinions, the greater the impact on their audience (Hovland, C. I., et. al., 1949; Hovland, C.I., 1957). Thus, the principle implies a potential strength for counselors which varies in terms of the way people feel about them after receiving their services.

C. To answer the question, **"How do people change their attitudes?"**, one must first define the concept "attitudes." The term attitudes, in this manual, refers to feelings for or against attitude objects. From a cognitive point of view, attitudes are extensions of one's belief system. Ultimately, they serve as the value base from which a person functions. To change an attitude, it is necessary to understand the psychological principles by which change becomes possible. For example, if a counselor wants to change the way a person thinks, he or she might use such techniques as: 1) Active Participation, 2) Cognitive Dissonance and/or 3) Induced Compliance.

1. *Active Participation:*
Active participation might include but certainly would not be restricted to such things as:

(a) Role Playing
(b) Role Reversal
(c) Role Observation

The principle is that permitting one to monitor his or her own behavior from a more objective point of view provides feedback which permits change.

**Importance to Counseling**: By having a client participate in role playing and/or role reversal exercises, the counselor can get the client to view himself or herself in action. Such an experience frequently motivates a desire for change.

2. *Cognitive Dissonance:*
Cognitive dissonance means that the cognition is at a distance. Whether or not it should remain at a distance is something the counselor must decide.

**Importance to Counseling**: A *male* student might say, "I hate school!" when in reality it is not school, perhaps not even the academic course work in school which he hates, but rather the social situations that take place *at school* that make coming to school distasteful to him. The counselor's first responsibility might be to help this student understand that it isn't school but the social situations at school that make him uncomfortable. By doing this, the counselor might get the student to withdraw his former statement, modify that statement or introduce a positive statement. If the counselor can help this student to recognize that it isn't the school which he hates, then the counselor has succeeded in bringing consonance (closeness) to a situation in which dissonance (distance) originally existed. The student can now feel free to like school but must deal with the social situations which are uncomfortable.

How does the counselor do this? The cognitively oriented counselor would assume that the person's behavior is based on faulty learning, incorrect inferences, incorrect information and/or the inability to distinguish between imagination and reality. The technique used in this case is juxtaposition, and what the counselor does is to juxtapose an ambiguous statement, i.e. a statement without any substantive base, "I hate school!" against the reality of the situation, i.e. the school is nothing more than a building with people in it. Since buildings are not protagonists nor antagonists, the student must be referring to the conditions which take place within the building. What takes place within a building involves people and is of an interpersonal and relating nature, and therefore must be treated that way. Thus, the student, through juxtaposition, i.e. through the use of sharp contrasts, understands that it is something within the school which he does not like. To find the exact protagonist or antagonist which creates the difficulty and discomfort, the counselor locates the onset of the difficulty by simply asking, "When did you first notice this feeling of discomfort?" followed by "What were you doing at that time . . . what was happening in your life?" With each question, the precise time at which the feeling first occurred and the feelings which precipitated those feelings of discomfort all come into play and thus define for the student (client) what it is that actually caused the discomfort. Once this is discovered, the counselor will want to help the student (client) overcome his feelings of discomfort. That can be done by following the protocols we have designed especially for counselors (see Section II).

3. *Induced Compliance:*

Before completing this section and going on to the next section, Procedures and Treatment Protocols, it seems important to point out that attitudinal change can also be brought about by *Induced Compliance* or getting someone to perform a counterattitudinal behavior through the use of incentives such as money. This, however, gets into positive, negative and generalized reinforcers which are part of theories of motivation.

**Importance to Counseling**: Induced compliance through the use of reinforcers such as money help the counselor to recognize alternatives by which people can be motivated.

D. To answer the question, **"How are people motivated?"** here are some of the ideas that will help counselors. Before a counselor can become an agent of change, it is important for that counselor to understand how to motivate people. Among the theories which are now prominent are: *Exchange Theory* (Blau, 1964); *Dissonance Theory* (Festinger, 1957); *Self Efficacy Theory* (Bandura, 1977) and *Game Theory* (Berne, 1964).

1. *Dissonance Theory:*

   Dissonance Theory reflects on how to change operational procedures. The idea is that psychological tension arises from nonfitting cognitions which seek resolution through additions and adaptations, i.e. a person experiences discomfort when he or she holds logically inconsistent cognitions about an object or event and is then motivated to reduce the dissonance through cognitive change. For examples of Festinger's (1957) Dissonance Theory in practice, see *Nexus Psychotherapy: Between Humanism and Behaviorism* (Gutsch & Ritenour, 1978).

2. *Self Efficacy Theory:*

   Self Efficacy Theory emerges from the work of Bandura (1977) and is based on the idea that people use those things which are effective for them. In effect, it emerges from (a) how people perceive their experiences, (b) how they evaluate the consequences of their experiences, and (c) how much exposure they have to standards modeled by others.

3. *Game Theory:*

   Game Theory (Berne, 1964) reflects on how a person functions to get what he or she wants. Examples of variations on Berne's original ideas might include the following (Trotzer, 1977)*:

   (a) **Avoidance Behaviors** — sometimes used by clients:

       (1) *Monopolizing* — when a client consumes all the counselor's time by talking about trivial things in an effort to control the counseling relationship.

       (2) *Hostility* — when a client attacks the counselor verbally so that he or she won't approach areas that the client does not want to talk about.

       (3) *Silence* — when a client refuses to say anything to the counselor so that the counselor can never learn what the client's deficits are.

---

*Copyright (c.) 1977. Permission to use the headings and/or subheadings in this section on Game Theory was granted by the Books/Cole Publishing Company.

(4) *Withdrawal* — when a client refuses to become involved in certain types of conversations with the counselor so that the most sensitive areas of the client's life are protected.

(5) *Absence* — when the client does not come to scheduled counseling sessions so that he or she can avoid interaction which may be frightening, embarassing or painful.

(6) *Intellectualizing* — when the client explains everything to a counselor in a logical way so that being responsible for those things he or she has done will not be so painful.

(7) *Displaced Humor* — when a client attempts to camouflage his or her real feelings through humor, i.e. when a client uses his or her sense of humor to create a situation in which the counselor cannot take him or her too seriously.

(b) **Manipulating Behaviors** — sometimes used by clients:

(1) *Scapegoating Behaviors* — when a client blames his or her family or anyone else in an effort to divert attention away from himself/herself and his or her defects, deficiencies or inappropriate actions.

(2) *Dependency* — when a client operates from a position of weakness, thus making everyone else responsible for solving his or her problems.

(3) *Submissiveness* — when a client attempts to gain dependency by appearing incapable of functioning, because he or she is so weak and fragile that he or she cannot help himself/herself.

(4) *Aggression* — when a client's hostility is directed toward others in an attempt to make others feel inferior. The objective is to gain control of a relationship by making others feel inadequate.

(c) **Helping Behaviors** — sometimes used by counselors:

(1) *Listening* — Counselor sometimes listen for themes which the person plays out through life experiences. Of extreme importance when listening is whether or not what the person says complements what the person is doing, and whether or not what the person is doing complements the coping skills of the person. Essentially what this means to the concept of counseling is that counselors must examine the incongruencies between cognitive sets, e.g. the interests, values, attitudes and objectives of the person, and the behaviors or acts produced as a result of those cognitive sets (Dember & Warm, 1979). Listening helps in the resolutions of difficulties because it helps the counselor to recognize incongruencies and plan intervention strategies which pave the way for congruencies.

(2) *Enabling* — Enablers are counselors who encourage clients (students) to reach out for new experiences but only after they have built effective backup systems.

(3) *Leading* — Counselors occasionally make suggestions as they help people to build coping skills and conflict resolution strategies; when that happens, the counselor is leading the person.

(4) *Self-Disclosure* — Counselors sometimes share their own personal experiences with their clients (the people they are serving professionally). When that happens, it is referred to as self-disclosure. Mowrer (1972) used the term to define the essence of his approach to group therapy (Integrity Therapy), and Jourard (1968) wrote a book about self-disclosure and its significance in counseling. Freud (Jones, 1955, p. 234) on the other hand, was critical of the technique and saw it as destructive; detrimental to the relationship because it seemed to destroy the analyst's control of the relationship. Freud thought that self disclosure on the part of the analyst would place the analyst in a position to be controlled by the patient. It now appears that self disclosure can be used effectively (Jourard, 1968). However, there are still some questions about when and/or under what conditions in the relationship, it should be initiated. Nevertheless, self disclosure, at best should help the client to understand that counselors, even as professionals, can and sometimes do have similar experiences. To this extent clients might understand that they're not alone.

(5) *Feedback* — This is a technique used by counselors to help clients understand where they are in a relationship. It is a disclosing technique which a counselor can use to express his or her feelings toward the client. If improperly used, it can be seen as a form of aggression, i.e. an attack on the client. It should, when used as a technique in counseling, be executed in the best interests of learning how to communicate what you see and understand as a "truth". That means that it is only your truth as you understand the situation and should not be communicated as an irreversible fact. For example, several months ago, a rather obese girl came in for counseling services. One of her concerns was that boys never asked her for dates. To implement a feedback-self-disclosure technique, the counselor asked her why she thought that happened. At first she responded by saying that she was not a sorority girl. She later said that she had a lot of studying to do and didn't really have time for boys. Finally, when the counselor said, "What else do you suppose it might

be?" she responded by saying, "Me! I look like hell and don't know what to do about it." Feedback is not always something you give to a person; it is sometimes a process contrived by a counselor to bring about self-understanding through self-disclosure. In this case, the girl responded to her innermost feelings. By so doing, the counselor was in a position to use a team approach consisting of a medical doctor (a nutritionist) and an expert on exercise. In a short period of time, the girl lost 35 pounds, and as a result, began to find life more congruent with her goals.

(6) *Leveling* — Counselors sometimes use a technique called leveling. This is an open, honest response to a client. It could be telling a person such as a heavy-set girl that she's fat. To do that, however, would be tactless. Therefore, although leveling is a direct way of handling a situation, it is not necessarily a discreet way of handling that situation. One example of leveling is illustrated in the following story: A man (a convict) who had been sentenced to prison for *pedophelia* (molesting children) requested counseling services. When talking with the counselor the client brought up the subject of his arrest and then proceeded to tell the counselor that he wasn't really guilty. The counselor said nothing and the man talked on — always denying his guilt. Suddenly, the counselor, who had to this point been looking away from the ex-convict, looked directly at him and said, "Yet, it seems that when so many people attest to something like this, it must be an idea with some foundation." The directness of his approach startled the man, who at first said nothing, and then suddenly started to cry while at the same time confessing that he couldn't control himself around little girls because they were so loving.

(d) **Emotional Behaviors** — sometimes used by clients:

(1) *Affection* — Clients will sometimes touch their counselors. At other times they may bring them presents or invite them to lunch. Such acts are occasionally seen as seductive. Naturally, in long term relationships, affection and warmth frequently increase. For this reason, the counselor should do his or her counseling in the office — not walking down the hall, not outside the building, and not on street corners. To deviate from the office setting is seldom in the best interests of the client and the relationship. Emotional balance is important to the client if he or she is to grow. Therefore, it is essential for the counselor to help the client develop self-identity, i.e. a feeling of autonomy within

the relationship. This can be done by constantly bringing the client to levels where risking change becomes possible. Remember, however, that clients should never risk change until they have a backup system and know how to use it.

(2) *Crying* — Crying has a powerful impact on people. Since counselors are people, it has an influence on them. To counter the impact it may have on counseling, counselors should be aware of the fact that crying is sometimes used as a coping strategy. It is done by some people when their options are limited or they have exhausted all other methods of coping with the situation in which they find themselves. It is important because it communicates a special message . . . it is a plea for help.

# SECTION II

# PROCEDURES AND TREATMENT
# PROTOCOLS

ALTHOUGH the understandings presented in Section I are important to counseling as a science, it is the protocols or intervention strategies by which a counselor puts his or her knowledge into action that become important to the practice of counseling. To help counselors in their efforts to work with clients, a number of procedures and treatment protocols are included in this manual. It should be noted that these protocols include some, but not necessarily all treatment considerations. This in no way suggests that these are the only treatment protocols nor that the facets of these protocols are the only considerations necessary for treatment.

The order of the protocols included in this section is as follows: Dating Behavior, Assertiveness-Training, Problem Solving-Decision Making, School Problems, Study Skills Training, Nail Biting, Obesity, Smoking, Stress, Speech Anxiety, Anxiety, Suicide Threat/Depression, and Obsessive-Compulsive Behavior.

# DATING BEHAVIOR

## I. Description

How often have you heard a male student say, "How do I ask a girl for a date? What do you talk about when you're on a date? or How do I know if a girl really likes me?" Dating is simply entering into a relationship with another person. In some ways it is like contract law, i.e. it is an agreement between two people to enter into a relationship based on certain specific stipulations. The agreement, in this case, is governed by personal objectives, values, interests and attitudes.

It seems reasonable to assume that large portions of any student body have some concerns about dating and it seems equally reasonable to believe that their concerns encompass such things as conditioned anxiety (being rejected), skills deficits (not knowing how to act or communicate) or faulty cognitive-evaluative appraisal (not being able to see something in proper perspective).

## II. Treatment Procedure

### A. *Assessment Phase*

Before you can help a client, the client has to state and define his or her problem. Tests such as the Speilberger (1973) State-Trait Anxiety Scale or Cattell's (1961) Anxiety Scale Questionnaire can be administered to determine how much, if any, anxiety is being experienced by the client. The deficit skills or strategies by which the client is coping can be observed by the client and the counselor. Essentially, however, dating is governed by three psychological principles, i.e. nearness, similarity, and reward. These three principles are of primary concern in dating. To be effective as a counselor, it is important to have the client understand how these principles work and how they impact relationships. This understanding should become a normal part of the treatment phase. That is, regardless of what techniques you might use, e.g. role playing and role reversal, it is important for the client to understand how these techniques relate to the three psychological principles which govern relationships.

### B. *Treatment Phase*

Through the use of such techniques as role playing, role reversal and/or role observation the counselor can help the client to clarify, evaluate and change his or her behavior. Changes in skill deficits are possible through rehearsal, i.e. the process of evaluation, instruction, modeling, practice, feedback, restructuring, and generalization.

The process involves a social skills approach and like Systematic Desensitization, falls into the category of models known as Behavior Theory. However, another approach to changing social behavior which seems to be gaining in popularity is the cognitive-behavioral approach. One of the most clearly illustrated approaches in this area belongs to Ellis (1973) who suggests that:

(a) Clients should be encouraged to look at the reality of what they are doing and saying in relationship experiences.

(b) Counselors should teach their clients, when necessary, the skills they need to improve their effectiveness.

(c) Counselors should assign tasks or give their respective clients homework assignments such as:

    (1) asking for a date if one is afraid to date, or

    (2) looking for a job if one has felt some inadequacies about himself or herself in searching for work.

(d) The counselor will do a good bit of the talking. Since the situation involves the client's belief system, Ellis feels that it is necessary to talk with the client in an effort to get the client to change that belief system.

(e) The counselor is didactic, i.e. the counselor is the teacher.

(f) The counselor must be a philosophical individual who can both establish change and represent (model) the change he or she is in the process of establishing.

(g) The counselor understands three basic things about his or her clients:

    (1) The present difficulties experienced by the client have antecedent causes.

    (2) The difficulties of the client continue because the client believes in the conditions which support these difficulties. In this case, because he believes such things as, "I am not good enough to date; No one could ever care for me; I can't learn to talk with girls; and/or Girls don't really care for me."

    (3) To overcome the difficult situation experienced by the client, the client must challenge his/her belief system.

What Ellis (1973) has attempted to do in establishing this treatment paradigm is to make the client:

(a) Aware of his/her negative thoughts and how they relate to social situations.

(b) Aware of how to become involved in change by first changing one's attitude (belief system).

(c) Aware of how to initiate those steps necessary to bring about change within one's own belief system.

(d) Aware of how to respond to nonverbal cues.

(e) Aware of how to enter into and terminate conversations.

(f) Aware of how to become more attractive, physically.

(g) Aware of the physical intimacy to which dating relationships can mutually lead.

III. **Sources of Further Information:**

Counselors who are looking for additional ideas on this subject might read:

Coleman, E. (1981). Counseling adolescent males. *The Personnel and Guidance Journal, 60*, 215-218.

Craighead, W. E., Kazdin, A. E., & Mahoney, M. J. (1976). *Behavior modification: Principles, issues, and applications.* Atlanta: Houghton Mifflin.

Curran, J.P., Gilbert, F. S., & Little, L. M. (1976). A comparison between behavioral replication training and sensitivity training approaches to heterosexual dating anxiety. *Journal of Counseling Psychology, 213*, 190-196.

Curran, J. P. (1977). Skills training as an approach to the treatment of heterosexual social anxiety: A review. *Psychological Bulletin, 84*, 140-157.

Ellis, A., & Grieger, R. (1977). *Handbook of rational-emotive therapy.* New York: Springer.

Glass, C. R., Gottman, J. M., & Shmurak, S. H. (1976). Response-acquisition and cognitive self-statement modification approaches to dating skills training. *Journal of Counseling Psychology, 23*, 520-526.

Hersen, M., Eisler, R. M., & Miller, P. M. (1979). *Progress in behavior modification.* New York: Academic.

Mandel, N. M., & Shrauger, J. S. (1980). The effects of self-evaluative statements on heterosocial approach in shy and nonshy males. *Cognitive Therapy and Research, 4*, 369-381.

# ASSERTIVENESS TRAINING

## I. Description

To be assertive is to be confident and to act with confidence. Thus, in this particular case, it is the counselor's goal to help his or her client to become assertive.

## II. Treatment Procedure

### A. *Assessment Phase*

Assessment is important in assertiveness training because it helps to clarify specific areas in which the training is essential. For example, the client may not have sufficient information to make a decision and thus, does not really know what to say or do. Second, the client may not know how to act (a behavioral deficit) or how to respond in an appropriate way. In these two cases, behavioral rehearsal might be appropriate.

However, the client might also experience negative anticipatory reactions, i.e. feelings of being rejected or evaluated. In such a case, the introduction of anxiety inducing stimuli in counter-position with an antagonist (relaxation) might be the most appropriate approach to treatment. That is, it might be good to teach the person how to relax each time the anxiety inducing situation is introduced.

Finally, the client might have been trained to believe that to be assertive is wrong. If this is true, then cognitive restructuring might be the most appropriate approach to treatment.

### B. *Treatment Phase*

**Step #1:** Help clients to recognize the need for change; help clients to become aware of who they are and how they can bring about change. Such an awareness is, in many cases, brought about through a figure-ground shift (the theoretical model from which the counselor draws at this point in the treatment, is a phenomenological approach). Once the client recognizes that a shift is possible (that change is possible), threatment will then progress to behavior rehearsal, i.e. getting the client to respond in more appropriate ways.

Rehearsals involving assertive behavior should be accompanied by feedback sessions involving those with whom the client is interacting; and counselors should emphasize the difference between assertiveness (a bold effort to make your point known) and aggressiveness (an attack on someone who holds a different point of view). This can all be done through the use of such techniques as role playing, role reversal and role observation.

**Step #2:** Designating target objectives is of primary importance. What the counselor frequently does in establishing a treatment paradigm is to select from a hierarchy of potentially assertive situations, those which appear to have the least resistance to change, i.e. the progress is always from those situations which are relatively simple to those which are more complex.

Rehearsals can, at first, be carried out with the counselor and later with others who agree to help in such training situations.

**Step #3:** Rehearsal and training should go beyond what the client has to say and should include nonverbal contingencies of human relating such as eye contact and voice control. However, all deficits should not be corrected at once. It is always more effective to start with the simple basic situations and graduate to the more difficult situations. The reason for this is that once clients have the opportunity to generalize from their counseling experiences to experiences outside of counseling, the reinforcement from the process of generalizing, i.e. moving from the safety of counseling experiences to the reality of real life experiences, gives clients the chance to be positively reinforced. Actually, the client has two problems. The first is to assert himself or herself in a specific situation. The second is to initiate his or her assertive behavior in an acceptable way, i.e. one in which he or she gains reinforcement. When clients change their behavior to become more effective in relationships the permanancy of this change will be influenced by how well that change is accepted by others.

**Step #4:** Clients should monitor all *in vivo* experiences dealing with change. Both the counselor and the client can then analyze any of the defects or deficiencies which might abort change. Thus, the counselor can schedule areas of training which appear most appropriate for the changes desired. Some counselors might think of this as assigning homework; others, however will think of it as monitoring and feedback sessions complemented by techniques designed to modify those behaviors which seem inappropriate to the situation.

### III. Sources for Further Information:

For those who are interested in gaining more information about this particular area of counselor intervention, you might read:

Alberti, R. E. (Ed.). (1977). *Assertiveness: Innovations, applications, issues.* San Luis Obispo, CA: Impact.

Alberti, R. E., & Emmons, M. L. (1978). *Your perfect right: A guide to assertiveness behavior* (3rd ed.). California: Impact.

Barron, J., & Hayashi, J. (1980). Shyness clinic: A social development program for adolescents and young adults. *The Personnel and Guidance Journal, 59,* 58-61.

Cormier, W. H., & Cormier, L. S. (1979). *Interviewing strategies for helpers: A guide to assessment, treatment, and evaluation.* Monterey, CA: Brooks/Cole.

Galassi, M. D., & Galassi, J. P. (1976). The effects of role playing variations on the assessment of assertive behavior. *Behavior Therapy, 7,* 343-347.

Goldfried, M. R., & Davidson, G. C. (1976). *Clinical behavior therapy.* New York:

Holt, Rinehart, & Winston.

Huey, W. C. (1983). Reducing adolescent aggression through group assertive training. *The School Counselor, 30,* 193-203.

Melnick, J., & Stocker, R. B. (1977). An experimental analysis of the behavioral rehearsal with feedback technique in assertiveness training. *Behavior Therapy, 8,* 222-228.

Sandmeyer, L. E., Ranck, A. W., & Chiswick, N. R. (1979). A peer assertiveness-training program. *The Personnel and Guidance Journal, 57,* 304-306.

# PROBLEM SOLVING — DECISION MAKING

## I. Description

Problem solving is sometimes thought of as a process, overt or covert, which provides a variety of potentially effective responses to problem situations. Supposedly, it increases the likelihood of selecting the most effective response from among various alternatives. Thus, making decisions wisely is an integral part of the counseling process and, in many respects, involves the teaching of specific problem solving skills. The basic goals of this approach are to improve coping effectiveness, i.e. problem solving skills within a wide variety of situations.

## II. Treatment Procedure

Treatment is usually systematic and includes the following steps:

### A. *Assessment Phase*

(a) General orientation — Assessment begins with a basic discussion of the rationale and anticipated benefits of treatment. This includes helping the client to understand (1) how he or she copes with situations at the present time, (2) how to identify problem situations when they occur, and (3) how to learn to respond discreetly in a problem situation.

(b) It also includes helping the client to understand how to develop a process for solving problems. Another means is by helping the client become sensitized to identifying problem situations. Some counselors find it helpful to assign homework which includes but is not restricted to such things as self-monitoring of daily living situations.

### B. *Treatment Phase*

**Step #1:** Problem definition and formulation — In this stage, the client learns to define external situations (stimuli) and internal situations (thoughts) which are involved in his or her problems. The client must also identify specific goals and the obstacles to reaching those goals.

**Step #2:** Generation of alternatives — Brainstorming is sometimes suggested as a key technique in generating alternative courses of action. When it is used, there are four basic rules to follow: (a) criticism and/or the judgment of ideas is done with discretion and never until the exercise or process is completed, (b) alternatives should never be rejected, no matter how wild they seem, (c) the greater the number of ideas, the better, and (d) the ability to combine and improve earlier ideas is the final goal.

**Step #3:** Discision making — The person determines which of the alternatives is worth pursuing by: (a) predicting the likely consequences of an action and (b) considering the utility of the consequences of such action. Once a strategy is chosen, it is necessary to develop as many alternative ways as possible to carry out the strategy. This is done by using the brainstorming process.

**Step #4:** Verification — The client must act on the decision so as to verify the actual effectiveness of the choice. If the strategy is not successful, it may reflect an inadequacy on the part of the client to carry out the skills necessary. When this happens, it may be necessary to return to brainstorming in an effort to develop other skills or strategies. If homework assignments are used, they should involve the use of problem solving techniques.

III. **Sources of Further Information:**

   For additional readings see:

France, M. H., & McDowell, C. (1983). A problem-solving paradigm: A preventive approach. *The School Counselor, 30*, 223-227.

Goldfried, M. R., & Davidson, G. C. (1976). *Clinical behavior therapy*. New York: Holt, Rinehart, & Winston.

Jepsen, D. A., Dusting, R., & Miars, R. (1982). The effects of problem-solving training on adolescents' career exploration and career decision making. *The Personnel and Guidance Journal, 61*, 149-153.

Lindbloom, G. (1981). A decision-making perspective on marital counseling: Issues and implications. *The School Counselor, 28*, 208-215.

# SCHOOL PROBLEMS

## I. Description

School problems, within the realm of counseling services, usually refer to poor academic performance based on handicaps, physiological and/or environmental influences, difficulties in adjustment, or difficulties with motivation. They may involve such things as speech problems, learning disabilities, mental retardation, emotional instability, behavior problems, social problems, cultural differences or medical problems. Clients (students) who have these problems usually comprise no more than 19% of the school age population and usually fall within the category of adolescents and preadolescents.

## II. Treatment Procedure

### A. *Assessment Phase*

**Step #1:** Review the client's (student's) school record and check for psychological information which may be helpful.

**Step #2:** With permission of the parents and support from your administrators, obtain assessment information about the parents, school, client, relatives and friends.

**Step #3:** Meet with parents if possible and encourage the parents to take the client to a physician to determine what, if any, organicity is involved.

**Step #4:** If necessary, explore the idea of having other specialists examining the client, i.e. professionals in such specialties as special education, developmental psychology, clinical psychology, speech and hearing, and school social worker.

**Step #5:** Compile information from all possible sources. Schedule a meeting with parents, school administrator(s), teacher(s), and client (if appropriate) and outline with them specific steps to be taken and objectives to be attained. Set specific goals which are within the range of the deficiency or defect of the client. For example,

(a) define the present level of the client's performance.

(b) define short range and long range goals for the client.

(c) define the specific educational and/or professional services to be provided as part of the treatment paradigm.

(d) stipulate when treatment will begin, how it will be monitored, by what criteria it will be monitored for effectiveness and when a second major assessment of the client will be made to determine progress.

### B. *Treatment Phase*

(a) If the client is experiencing stress or anxiety, short term counseling might be appropriate.

(b) If the problem is appropriate, group counseling might be used.

### C. *Treatment Paradigm*

**Consideration #1:** A treatment paradigm might include an approach something like Fritz Redl's (1966) Life Space Interview. In it, he attempts to provide a climate in which the client (student) can discuss his or her fears, a climate in which there is some emphasis on how to make choices wisely, a climate in which the client becomes aware of the consequences of his or her behavior before it is initiated, and a climate in which the client can understand how to use his or her skills in the best ways possible.

**Consideration #2:** A treatment paradigm might include something like Bersoff's and Grieger's (1971) psychosituational interviews in which the counselor examines the attitude of those who might be creating undue pressure on the client (student).

**Consideration #3:** Still another treatment paradigm which might be of interest to counselors is one which involves role playing, role reversal and/or role observation. These techniques are helpful as a means of enabling clients (students) to gain some awareness of how they are impacting the lives of those around them.

**NOTE:** The counselor, in this case, serves both as a facilitator of information and as a consultant. Ultimately he or she can be expected to (a) counsel with, consult about, or refer the client, (b) help parents to understand and learn more about parenting, (c) set up a client management plan, (d) introduce bibliotherapy when necessary, i.e. the introduction of books and other reading materials designed to educate parents in their role of helping their children to adjust to the problems encountered in school.

## III. Sources of Further Information

Additional information can be found by reading:

Allen, J. E., Guruaj, V. J., & Russo, R. W. (1977). *Practical points in pediatrics* (2nd ed.). New York: Medical Examinations Publishing.

Bersoff, D. N., & Grieger, R. M. (1971). An interview model for the psychosituational assessment of children's behavior. *American Journal of Orthopsychiatry, 41,* 483-493.

Epstein, R., & Goss, C. M. (1978). A self control procedure for the maintenance of nondisruptive behavior in an elementary school. *Behavior Therapy, 9,* 109-117.

Rosen, M., & Arsht, E. D. (1979). *Psychological approaches to family practice: A primary care manual.* Baltimore: University Park Press.

Walker, H. M., Hops, H., & Fiegenhaum, E. (1976). Deviant classroom behavior as a function of social and token cost contingency. *Behavior Therapy, 7,* 76-88.

# STUDY SKILLS TRAINING

## I. Description

Study skills training is a process designed to help people learn how to study. Since many clients (students) have difficulty with handling and ingesting large quantities of information efficiently, study skills training has been one method of exposing them to techniques which might be helpful. One such technique is known as contingency management.

## II. Treatment Procedure

### A. *Assessment Phase*

Assessment is made by observing the person directly. The counselor knows what deficits he or she has observed and how to use this data as a baseline to measure change. As study skills change, the counselor also measures changes in outcome (results of the new skills introduced).

### B. Treatment Phase

Contingency management includes the following steps:

**Step #1:** Self-Observation — For the first week the counselor asks clients to keep a daily written record of study time and place. This is used as a baseline against which to evaluate change in study behavior.

**Step #2:** Stimulus Control — Where to study may have an effect on the quality of study time. Suggestions on where to study include: (a) choosing a place which is free from distractions and interruptions, (b) studying in a place with adequate lighting, and (c) setting up a regular study schedule.

Self-observation may indicate that the client studies more effectively during certain times of the day and/or in specific areas. An accurate assessment of environmental stimuli will help to identify key areas which need to be modified or changed.

**Step #3:** Educate the client in how to study the SQ3R Method (Survey, Question, Read, Recitation, Review). The following is one system of doing this: (a) go through reading assignments and underline anything that appears to be highlighted in the chapter, i.e. such things as italicized words, quotes, bold headings and graphs; (b) try to get an idea of the organization of the chapter, focus on headings and subheadings to determine the purpose and sequence of the material, read chapter summaries before reading the chapter, and turn a chapter heading into a question; (c) read actively; (d) recite; and (e) review (Rimm & Masters, 1979, p. 437).

**Step #4:** Contingency Management — The client and the counselor identify specific reinforcers to be applied following the implementation of preselected study skill behaviors. Self-monitoring procedures are used to assess client improvement of the identified behaviors. The client and the counselor develop a contract agreement that includes a method for improving study skills, monitoring procedures to be used to evaluate progress, and the specific positive and/or negative reinforcers to be used in contingency management.

III. **Sources of Further Information:**

For additional information, read:

Dobbins, J. E. (1982). *How to take a test*. Princeton: Educational Testing Service.

Greiner, J. M., & Karoly, P. (1976). Effects of self-control training on study activity and academic performance: An analysis of self-monitoring, self-reward, and systematic planning components. *Journal of Counseling Psychology, 23*, 495-502.

Harris, A. J. (1979). *Everything you ever wanted to know about good study habits (and were afraid to ask)*. Unpublished manuscript, University of Southern Mississippi, University Counseling Center, Hattiesburg, MS.

Hefferman, T., & Richards, C. S. (1981). Self-control of study behavior: Identification and evaluation of natural methods. *Journal of Counseling Psychology, 28*, 361-364.

Krumboltz, J. D., & Thoresen, C. E. (1976). *Counseling methods*. New York: Holt, Rinehart & Winston.

Rimm, D. C., & Masters, J. C. (1979). *Behavior therapy*. New York: Academic.

Robyak, J. E. (1977). A revised study skills model: Do some of them practice what we teach? *The Personnel and Guidance Journal, 56*, 171-175.

# NAIL BITING

## I. Description

Nail biting is a habit. Whether or not you consider it good or bad is probably relative to what the alternatives might be. At the present time, there are a number of techniques which have been used to counter this condition. Among them are such treatment strategies as negative practice, electric shock, cue-controlled relaxation, hypnotic suggestion, positive reinforcement and aversive conditioning (placing a substance, bitter to the taste, on the nails).

## II. Treatment Procedures

### A. *Assessment Phase*

Assessment is sometimes done by measuring the nails. The length of the nails at the beginning of treatment then serves as the baseline against which change can be measured.

### B. *Treatment Phase*

One of the most effective treatment procedures is self-monitoring. When self-monitoring is used in combination with the substitution of incompatible responses, i.e. teaching the client a response pattern which is not compatible with nail biting, the results are quite good.

**Step #1:** The counselor begins by asking the nail biter to record (by making a check mark on a 3 x 5 index card) each nail biting experience. The card is then turned over to the counselor who graphs the results. This process continues throughout the treatment and provides a data base from which the counselor and client can determine what progress, if any, is being made.

**Step #2:** The length of each nail is measured from the base (center most portion) to the top. This provides a second data base from which to measure progress. It is important to establish both baselines, i.e. frequency of nail biting and length of nails, before initiating treatment. To assume exactness in data, the assessments should probably be made on a daily basis for one week.

**Step #3:** When the person (client) bites his or her nails, he or she is instructed to engage immediately in a response pattern which is incompatible with nail biting, socially inconspicuous, and compatible with ongoing activities. Say, for example, that the person is watching television and suddenly starts biting his or her nails. One response pattern which is incompatible with nail biting and is socially acceptable is to eat peanuts. This, then, might be what the client elects to do. Another technique might be to have clients place their hands down at their sides, clench their fists and squeeze until tension is felt.

III. **Sources of Further Information:**

For those who are interested, additional information can be found in the following articles:

Adesso, V. J., Vargas, J. M., & Siddall, J. W. (1979). Role of awareness in reducing nail-biting behavior. *Behavior Therapy, 10,* 148-154.

Azrin, N. H., & Nunn, R. G. (1973). Habit-reversal: A method of eliminating nervous habits and tics. *Behavior Research and Therapy, 11,* 619-628.

Davidson, A. (1976). Sensitization and information for nailbiting. *Behavior Therapy, 7,* 512-518.

Delparto, D. J., Aleh, E., Bambush, I., & Barclay, L. A. (1977). Treatment of fingernail biting by habit reversal. *Journal of Behavior Therapy and Experimental Psychology, 8,* 319-320.

# OBESITY

## I. Descrition

Obesity is generally recognized as a major health problem although there is little general agreement as to a precise means for determining exactly who is obese. It is sometimes regarded as a condition involving excessive fat or adipose tissue in the body mass.

An analysis of the current literature regarding the treatment of obesity favors behavioral techniques over other treatment modalities. Most behavioral programs have employed one or more of the following components: (a) self-monitoring of body weight and/or food intake, (b) implicit or explicit goal setting, (c) nutritional, exercise, and health counseling, (d) tangible operant consequences, (e) covert conditioning and cognitive restructuring techniques, (f) self-presented consequences, (g) and stimulus control procedures.

## II. Treatment Procedure

### A. *Assessment Phase*

Assessment is usually made by weighing the client. The weight at which the client begins treatment then serves as the baseline against which to measure change.

### B. *Treatment Phase*

Treatment for the obese person usually begins with instructions on how to keep a daily log of the amount of food eaten. This includes the number of calories consumed. The client must weigh at the same time each week. This self-monitoring procedure will not only provide baseline data, but will also allow the counselor to measure progress objectively. The treatment procedure involves a multiple step approach:

**Step #1:** Initiate an appropriate self-monitoring procedure. Although self-monitoring is used as an assessment tool, it is also an effective treatment procedure.

**Step #2:** Implement an exercise plan. This should be a realistic plan using gradual increments of exercise requirements. The activities should be enjoyable for the client. A physician should be involved when the client has health problems.

**Step #3:** Use the help of a physician to design a special diet for the client. That is, refer the person to a medical doctor of *his or her choice, with his or her permission* and for the purpose of having a doctor prescribe a diet.

**Step #4:** The counselor should implement stimulus control measures. Essentially, stimulus control methods are used to teach the obese individual how to achieve control of his or her eating habits. Specific stimulus control procedures include:

(a) Separate eating from all other activities. Eat in a specific room and at designated times and do not engage in any other activities while eating nor such things as television viewing or reading.

(b) Make sure that high-calorie foods are unavailable; don't buy high calorie foods.

(c) Alter food portions, i.e use small plates and shallow bowls. Surplus food should be stored prior to eating.

(d) Eat slowly, i.e. swallow one bite before preparing for the next. Food utensils should be put down between bites.

(e) Avoid waste eating. Don't eat something simply because it has been paid for or would otherwise be thrown out. Set aside small portions of each food item at the beginning of each meal and leave these to be thrown out, i.e. the client should not "clean" his or her plate.

The goal of each of these steps, of course, is to restrict both the range and frequency of the cues associated with overeating.

III. **Sources of Further Information:**

For additional reading see:

Chapman, S., & Jeffrey, D. B. (1979). Processes in maintenance of weight loss with behavior therapy. *Behavior Therapy, 10,* 566-570.

Coates, T. J., & Thoresen, C. E. (1981). Behavior and weight change in three obese adolescents. *Behavior Therapy, 12,* 363-399.

Dunkel, L. D., & Glaros, A. G. (1978). Comparison of self-instruction vs. stimulus control treatments for obesity. *Cognitive Therapy and Research, 2,* 75-78.

Kingsley, R. G., & Shapiro, J. (1977). A comparison of three behavioral programs for control of obesity in children. *Behavior Therapy, 8,* 30-36.

Leitenberg, H. (1976). *Handbook of behavior modification and behavior therapy.* Englewood Cliffs, NJ: Prentice-Hall.

Weiss, A. R. (1977). A behavioral approach to the treatment of adolescent obesity. *Behavior Therapy, 8,* 720-726.

Wheeler, M. E., & Hess, K. W. (1976). Treatment of juvenile obesity by successive approximation control of eating. *Journal of Behavior Therapy and Experimental Psychiatry, 7,* 235-241.

# SMOKING

## I. Description

Smoking is usually referred to as a habit. Naturally, it is always important to distinguish between an addiction and a habit. Thus, the counselor should know that addiction is characterized by:

(a) An overwhelming desire or compulsion to use or take a substance.
(b) A tendency to increase the dosage because one's tolerance increases with use, thus making it necessary to take more of the substance to get the same effect.
(c) Psychological and physiological dependency on the substance . . . the latter being manifest in withdrawal symptoms when the substance is not used for a period of time.

With a habit, the person has a desire but not a compulsion to take the substance, little or no tendency to increase the dosage and a psychological but not a physiological dependency on the substance.

Why do people smoke? No one really knows but it seems that some young people smoke to emulate their parents; some people seem to smoke because it gives them something to do with their hands when they are at a social function; others seem to smoke because it gives them a sense of identity; and still others seem to smoke to relieve tension. Whatever the reason, the problem is a tough one to solve. The difficulty seems to lie with the fact that the person is pairing a condition, such as tension, with an act, such as smoking. When this happens, regardless of how inadvertent the intent may be, the person is involved in the process of conditioning. That is, the person is pairing tension reduction with smoking. When repeated for any length of time, the result is cigarette addiction. This addiction can then serve as a basis for second order learning. That is, a condition is brought about by presenting two contingencies contiguously. At first the person smokes a cigarette and drinks coffee. Soon the condition changes and each time the person drinks coffee, he or she smokes a cigarette. Another example of second order learning occurs when the person smokes a cigarette and relaxes in his or her favorite chair. Soon, every time the person sits in this favorite chair he or she lights up a cigarette.

## II. Treatment Procedure

### A. *Assessment Phase*

The person seeking assistance usually reports cigarette consumption to the counselor. The counselor then uses the figure as a baseline against which to measure change.

### B. *Treatment Phase*

One program of treatment with which counselors and psychologists have reported some success consists of five (5) weekly sessions. The sessions last from 30 to 90 minutes and the following three (3) treatment steps are involved:

**Step #1:** The counselor and client plan for a change. This change begins by having the smoker self-monitor (log) the time, place, activity and perceived feeling which accompanies smoking. Such data provide baseline information for the smoker and thus make the smoker aware of the frequency with which smoking occurs. It should be noted that if the smoker is asked for an estimate of this data, it is likely that smoking will actually decrease following instructions to monitor, i.e. smoking will decrease as recognition increases.

The second counseling session with the smoker can then be devoted to describing a general approach to treatment; a discussion of the reasons for smoking and an examination of feelings attached to smoking can now be pursued. Possible alternative behaviors (substitute behaviors for smoking) can be investigated as part of developing a problem-solving model for the cessation of smoking in which the *urge to smoke* becomes the stimulus for implementing a problem solving technique. Thus, the smoker must first be encouraged to:

(a) Identify and define those factors which stimulate (create an urge for) smoking.

(b) Consider alternatives to smoking which might neutralize the urge — (one of our friends substitutes chewing tobacco for smoking — that's probably a poor alternative).

(c) Test those alternatives against reality (see if they really work).

(d) Practice viable alternatives until they become part of a well established nonsmoking life style.

**Step #2:** A number of new treatment procedures now exist which give the smoker some alternatives to smoking. Among the most recent developments in clinical pharmacology is *Nicorette* (a nicotine resin complex) manufactured by Merrell Dow Pharmaceuticals, Incorporated. Nicorette is available in the form of chewing gum. The gum is supposed to be sugar free and suitable for *most* denture wearers. The treatment must be administered by a medical doctor because there is some concern about how it impacts people who have coronary heart disease, cardiac arrhythmia, or vasospastic disease.* In a recent study by Jarvis, Raw, Russell, and Feyerabend (1982) they compared the effectiveness of a nicotine chewing gum with a placebo and found that the nicotine chewing gum worked quite well. Of 58 subjects given the active gum, 27 were not smoking at the end of one year.

---

*NOTE: Counselors should have a list of medical doctors to whom they can refer clients. The list should be based on a personal understanding of each doctor's skills and a personal agreement with each doctor to take referrals.

Other treatment techniques such as satiation smoking are also available to the smoker. Both concepts however *must be supervised by a medical doctor*.

**Step #3:** Step number 3 is aimed at maintaining change. Nonsmoking in this case is seen as the result of alternatives to smoking. The composite of alternatives may include relaxation techniques, exercising techniques and/or cognitive techniques.

**NOTE:** Because smoking to a cadence (rapid smoking) does stress the cardiovascular system, i.e. it increases heart rate, blood pressure and carboxyhemoglobin levels, the cadence smoking treatment paradigm should not be set up without constant monitoring by a physician who is familiar with the technique and is willing to work with the counselor.

III. **Sources of Further Information:**

For additional information read:

Flaxman, J. (1978). Quitting smoking now or later: Gradual, abrupt, immediate, and delayed quitting. *Behavior Therapy, 9*, 260-270.

Jarvis, M. J., Raw, M., Russell, M. A. H., & Feyerabend, C. (1982). Randomised controlled trial of nicotine chewing-gum. *British Medical Journal, 285*, 537-540.

Lando, H. A. (1978). Toward a clinically effective paradigm for maintenance of nonsmoking. *Behavior Therapy, 9*, 666-668.

Leichtenstein, E., Harris, D. E., Birchler, G. R., Wahl, J. M., & Schmal, D. P. (1973). Comparison of rapid smoking, warm-smoky air, and attention placebo in the modification of smoking behavior. *Journal of Consulting and clinical Psychology, 40*, 92-98.

Lublin, I., & Joslyn, L. (1968, September). *Aversive conditioning of cigarette addiction*. Unpublished paper presented at the meeting of the American Pscyhological Association, San Francisco, CA.

Perri, M. G., Richards, C. S., & Schulfheis, K.K. (1977). Behavioral self-control and smoking reduction: A study of self-initiated attempts to reduce smoking. *Behavior Therapy, 8*, 360-365.

# STRESS

## I. Description

Stress is the non-specific response of the body to any demand (Selye, 1978, p. 58). What this means is that a certain set of changes occur in an organism or a person when the organism or person experiences stressors, i.e. conflict, pressure, tension, or perhaps even pleasure.

## II. Treatment Procedures

### A. *Assessment Phase*

Assessment of stress is physiological and can be assessed through medical referral.

### B. *Treatment Phase*

One method of treating stress is referred to as stress inoculation training. Stress inoculation training is a process designed to help a client learn how to develop coping skills in an effort to deal with stressful situations. It functions in much the same way as medical inoculation, i.e. resistance is created by exposing the client to a stimulus strong enough to arouse body defenses but not strong enough to overwhelm him or her. Similarly, stress inoculation training provides psychological protection by helping the person to develop skills and strategies to deal with conditions which normally create stress. The treatment involves four major steps:

**Step #1:** Educate the client regarding stress and review the procedures for stress inoculation training with him or her.

**Step #2:** Introduce and rehearse direct action coping strategies. Examples of direct action coping are identification of escape routes, mental relaxation techniques, and physical relaxation techniques. The client should be allowed to choose which strategy he or she feels is most appropriate.

**Step #3:** Educate the client in the four phases of cognitive coping:

(a) Preparing for the situation.
(b) Confronting and handling the situation.
(c) Coping with critical moments.
(d) Reinforcing oneself after the situation.

In acquiring the cognitive strategies it is helpful for the counselor to model coping thoughts. It is also important for the client to select and practice appropriate coping thoughts.

**Step #4:** The final step involves the application of all coping strategies to the problem situation. This may be initiated through several techniques, some of which are modeling, role playing, and homework assignments.

III. **Sources of Further Information:**

For additional information see:

Barrow, J. C., & Prosen, S. S. (1981). A model of stress and counseling intervention. *The Personnel and Guidance Journal, 60,* 5-10.

Bayerl, J. A., & MacKenzie, T. E. (1981). Unload, don't overload: A workshop on stress in education. *The School Counselor, 29,* 54-60.

Cormier, W. H., & Cormier, L. S. (1979). *Interviewing strategies for helpers: A guide to assessment, treatment, and evaluation.* Monterey, CA: Brooks/Cole.

Klingman, A. (1978). Children in stress: Anticipatory guidance in the framework of the educational system. *The Personnel and Guidance Journal, 57,* 22-26.

O'Rear, J. M., & Hope, K. (1979). Coping with stress: Getting the message across. *The Personnel and Guidance Journal, 57,* 556-557.

Sparks, D., & Ingram, M. J. (1979). Stress prevention and management: A workshop approach. *The Personnel and Guidance Journal, 58,* 197-200.

# SPEECH ANXIETY

## I. Description

The anxiety one develops over assignments to do public speaking is probably a form of fear. A review of the current research regarding treatment procedures for speech anxiety indicates that numerous techniques have been attempted with varying degrees of success. Commonly used treatment strategies include systematic desensitization, rational emotive therapy (RET), stress inoculation training, skills training, *in vivo* flooding, and various combinations of these. The treatment procedure which appears to be most widely used and has met with some success is a combination of cognitive restructuring (RET) and skills training.

Cognitive restructuring techniques reduce anxiety while exposing the client to anxiety management skills. Skills training focuses on teaching the individual to make competent responses and makes no direct effort to decondition anxiety. Such an approach should result in better performance, more positive feedback as a result of the performance, fewer negative self-statements, and thus, less anxiety in speech situations.

## II. Treatment Procedure

### A. *Assessment Phase*

Assessment baselines can be established by monitoring physiological, cognitive, and behavioral responses. Physiological responses such as sweating, shaking, and rapid heart rate can be measured by using the galvanic skin response. Self-monitoring of cognitions can be measured by using Rational Emotive Therapy (RET) techniques and behavioral responses can be measured by establishing specific criteria which are in conflict with the anxiety one has over public speaking. None of the treatments for speech anxiety is effective with all people. Thus, an assessment of physiological, cognitive, and behavioral responses should provide the information necessary for selecting the appropriate treatment procedure.

### B. *Treatment Phase*

Since skills training and RET combined have proven to be successful in reducing speech anxiety, the counselor might best consider these intervention strategies first. RET postulates that maladaptive feelings of anxiety such as those experienced in speech anxiety are the result of irrational themes. Among the irrational themes Ellis (1973) labels, the three most common are: (a) everyone must love or like me in all situations, (b) I must be competent and successful in all situations, and (c) when life is not the way I want, it is awful and upsetting. Once the themes are identified, they are logically challenged and replaced with more rational ones. RET also assumes that an individual maladaptive emotional response reflects an indiscriminate and automatic labeling of a situation. Although the emotional reaction may be appropriate to the label one attaches to a situation, the label itself may be basically in-accurate. These labels need to be identified, challenged, and replaced with more rational ones. Homework involving self-monitoring and practice is a vital part of RET.

Skills training of speech anxious people focuses on teaching the skills necessary for successful performance. Through assessment, skill deficiencies or behavioral excesses are identified and become the target of treatment. Common skill deficits in speech anxiety include; (a) pac-ing, (b) swaying, (c) shuffling feet, (d) trembling knees, (e) extraneous arm and hand movements, (f) extraneous head movements, (g) re-strained hands, (h) lack of eye contact, (i) tense face muscles, (j) flat af-fect, (k) moist lips, (l) difficulties swallowing, (m) clearing throat, (n) heavy breathing, (o) quivering voice, and (p) speech blocks.

Techniques used in alleviating these deficits include: (a) behavioral rehearsal, (b) modeling, (c) coaching, (d) feedback — including video-tape replays, (e) reinforcement, and (f) homework.

III. **Sources of Further Information:**

For additional information, read:

Auerback, A. (1981). Self-administered treatments of public speaking anxiety. *The Personnel and Guidance Journal, 60*, 106-109.

Ellis, A. (1973). *Humanistic psychotherapy: The rational-emotive approach.* New York: Julian.

Fremouw, W. J., & Scott, M. D. (1979). Cognitive restructuring: An alternative method for the treatment of communication apprehension. *Communication Education, 28*, 129-133.

Fremouw, W. J., & Zitter, R. E. (1978). A comparison of skills training and cognitive restructuring-relaxation for the treatment of speech anxiety. *Behavior Therapy, 9*, 248-259.

Goldfried, M. R., & Davidson, G. C. (1976). *Clinical behavior therapy.* New York: Holt, Rinehart, & Winston.

# ANXIETY

## I. Description

Anxiety is frequently recognized as fear without an object or tension which stems from anticipation. Although the fear object cannot be identified or defined, there are feelings of uneasiness and tension within the person. Fear, on the other hand, is an emotional response to a consciously recognized external threat.

The anxiety experience contains four parts (Lighthall, 1964):

(a) anxiety cue
(b) anxiety affect
(c) primary anxiety reaction
(d) adaptive anxiety reaction (p. 5)

Anxiety cue serves as a thought, idea or experience which precipitates anxiety affect. Anxiety affect, in turn, is a surge of emotion which demands relief because of the tension it creates. Primary anxiety reaction is a strategic or defensive reaction by which the person attempts to cope with tension. It may include physical escape or diversionary strategies, e.g. an attempt to think about something else. Adaptive anxiety reaction, the fourth part of this sequence, occurs less frequently because it requires the courage to examine the condition and to seek an answer.

## II. Treatment Procedure

Systematic desensitization is one method of treatment. This treatment paradigm was originally introduced by Joseph Wolpe (1952; 1954; 1969). It consists of intervention efforts on the part of the counselor or therapist to counter the condition recognized as anxiety. It is used with people who are rational in many of their everyday activities, but perform poorly in other situations because they anticipate from previous encounters with their environments things which are not necessarily there now. Systematic, by definition, means the gradual and systematic application of treatment. Desensitization, by definition, means reducing the person's anxiety. The two ideas, when placed side by side, tell you that anxiety is being reduced in a systematic way through the gradual application of treatment, i.e. relaxation is counterposed with the fear object in a sequence of steps until the anxiety is extinguished.

A. *Assessment Phase*

1. *Hierarchies* — To be systematic in the application of relaxation, Wolpe (1969) used a number of assessment techniques to help his clients define those areas of fear which were most disturbing to them. Ultimately, these assessment techniques, e.g. the Willoughby Questionnaire, the Medical Interview, Wolpe's Fear Schedule and his probing techniques as they relate to unadaptive anxiety, were used to discover which anxiety evoking experiences were the lowest

in anxiety producing contingencies and which the highest. He then scaled these experiences according to what he referred to as *SUDS* (subjective units of disturbance). His reason for doing this was so that he could start his therapy by counterposing the antagonist — relaxation — with the lowest anxiety inducing experience on the scale. Understanding the degree of disturbance generated by each subject unit permitted him to work sequentially up to those experiences which produced the greatest anxiety.

B. *Treatment Phase*

1. *Relaxation* — Paramount in this model is the idea of progressive relaxation. Relaxation serves as an antagonist to anxiety, i.e. a person cannot relax and be anxious at the same time. Therefore, the first step in treatment is to train the person to relax. Since Wolpe gained much of his knowledge about relaxation from Jacobson (1938), it might be a good idea to read Jacobson's book, *Progressive Relaxation*, in order to develop a more comprehensive understanding of how important the concept is to counseling.

2. *Desensitization* — Desensitization involves the process of selecting the most appropriate scaled anxiety experiences to counterpose with relaxation. To do this, Wolpe instructed the patient to imagine a fear situation covertly and raise his or her index finger when his (Wolpe's) descriptions of that experience induced fear. He then asked the patient to rate the fear on a basis of 0-100, with "0" representing no fear, and "100" representing a great deal of fear. By using this technique, he developed a method of monitoring the fear extensiveness experienced by his patients.

3. *Key components of the Model*:

    (a) Identification of the Hierarchy (fear) Items. These items should elicit a range of emotional responses from the client.

    (b) Identification of Control (non-fear) Items. These items are used to test the client's ability to assume an "anxiety-free" state.

    (c) Ranking and spacing of items according to their anxiety producing order.

    (d) The counter posing of relaxation and anxiety evoking stimuli as an antagonist.

**NOTE:** In practice, regardless of what the antagonist may be, the client and counselor agree on a system by which the client can communicate feelings of anxiousness or calmness. The counselor then verbally introduces anxiety inducing scenes in a systematic way (from least fearful to most fearful). The counselor protects the client by counter posing an antagonist during any scene which produces extensive anxiety. This gradual introduction of anxiety inducing scenes accompanied by the counter positioning of an antagonist when the scenes create excessive amounts of anxiety provides the client with a systematic approach to the desensitization of his or her anxiety.

A scene may last for a number of minutes before inducing fear. Once fear is induced, the counselor tells the client to "shut-off" the scene and then introduces the antagonist. If the antagonist is relaxation, the counselor will take the client (person) into deep muscle relaxation techniques whenever anxiety is experienced.

Systematic desensitzation is derived from Behavior Therapy and as such is part of the behavioral model. This is not the only way to treat anxiety, but it is one way of treating anxiety which has been well researched.

### A Word of Caution

Typically, the person experiencing anxiety has some of the following characteristics: paces the floor, cannot sleep well, feels apprehensive, experiences low self-worth, has an unsettled feeling in his or her stomach, sweats profusely, experiences palpitations, feels shaky, feels nauseated, feels "light headed," is confused, has dilated pupils, has to urinate frequently, has diarrhea, and experiences cold hands and feet.

Since there are a number of medical orientations which resemble anxiety, we caution the counselor to refer the person with these symptoms for medical help. Among the medical illnesses with similar syndromes are:

(a) **Hyperthyrodisim** — a condition in which an overactive thyroid gland causes:
   (1) warm sweat (not cold sweat)
   (2) a loss of weight (usually while food intake increases)
   (3) feelings of anxiousness
   (4) rapid heartbeat
   (5) tremors (shaking)
   (6) thinning hair (rapid onset)
(b) **Hyperventilation** — a condition caused by a depletion of carbon dioxide. The person experiences:
   (1) numbness
   (2) tingling of the fingertips, and sometimes hands and feet (paresthesias)
   (3) "light-headedness"
   (4) dizziness
   (5) chest pains
Typically the person experiencing this condition will be a female between 12 and 40 years of age.

(c) **Chronic kidney disease** — a condition in which the kidneys no longer function the way they should and the person experiences such things as:
    (1) irritability
    (2) depression
    (3) feelings of anxiousness
    (4) nausea
    (5) constipation

(d) **Heart attack** — a condition in which the heart fails to perform as it should and the person experiences such things as:
    (1) sweating
    (2) chest pains
    (3) paresthesias
Typically the person experiencing this condition is a male 45 years of age or older.

(e) **Hypoglycemia** — a condition in which the blood sugar of the person is low and the person experiences such things as:
    (1) feelings of anxiousness
    (2) headaches
    (3) sweating
    (4) tremors (shaky)

(f) **Postconcussion syndrome** — a condition in which the person has had a head or whiplash injury and as a result experiences such things as:
    (1) headaches
    (2) irritability
    (3) hypersensitivity to noise
    (4) hypersensitivity to light
    (5) hypersensitivity to heat
    (6) chronic fatigue

(g) **Tuberculosis** — a communicable disease condition which usually affects the lungs and results in such experiences as:
    (1) chest pains
    (2) sweating (especially night sweating)
    (3) weight loss
    (4) chronic fatigue
    (5) excessive coughing

(h) **Pheochromocytoma** — a tumor which alters epinephrine and norepinephrine and causes such things as:
    (1) anxious feelings
    (2) sweating
    (3) headaches

(4) nervousness

(5) tremors

(6) nausea

(7) weakness

(8) chest pain

(9) impaired vision

III. **Sources of Further Information:**

For further reading see:

Cormier, W. H., & Cormier, L. S. (1979). *Interviewing strategies for helpers: A guide to assessment, treatment, and evaluation*. Monterey, CA: Brooks/Cole.

Goldfried, M. R., & Davidson, G. C. (1976). *Clinical behavior therapy*. New York: Holt, Rinehart & Winston.

Lighthall, F. F. (1964). *Anxiety as related to thinking and forgetting*. Washington: National Education Association (What research says to the teacher — series #30).

Murphy, K. C. (1980). A cognitive-behavioral approach to client anxiety, anger, depression and guilt. *The Personnel and Guidance Journal, 59*, 202-205.

Small, L. (1970). *The briefer psychotherapies*. New York: Brunner/Mazel.

Trimble, R. W., & Carter, C. A. (1980). Test anxiety workshops using undergraduates as leaders. *The Personnel and Guidance Journal, 59*, 173-175.

Wolpe, J. (1952). Objective psychotherapy of the neurosis. *South African Medical Journal, 26*, 825.

Wolpe, J. (1954). Reciprocal inhibition as the main basis of psychotherapeutic effects. *Archives of Neurological Psychiatry, 72*, 205.

Wolpe, J. (1958). *Psychotherapy by reciprocal inhibition*. Stanford, CA: Stanford University Press.

Wolpe, J. (1969). *The practice of behavior therapy*. New York: Pergamon.

# SUICIDE THREAT/DEPRESSION

## I. Description

Suicide is sometimes accompanied by or preceded by periods of depression. Characteristically, depression is defined by:

(a) *Alterations in mood*, i.e. lack of interest, loneliness, crying spells and sadness.

(b) *Negative self-concept*, i.e. not feeling good about one's accomplishments . . . feelings of failure.

(c) *Psychomotor retardation*, i.e. a slowing down of the thought process . . . a diminished interest in life.

(d) *Feelings of helplessness*, i.e. feelings of inadequacy and hopelessness.

(e) *Feelings of anxiety*, i.e. feelings of anxiousness

(f) *Diminished social relations*, i.e. withdrawal from social contact, isolation and a general lack of interest in fraternizing.

## II. Treatment Precedure

### A. *Assessment Phase — By Telephone or in Person*

An assessment of a person's potential for suicide can be made by looking at the person's general pattern of responding and comparing it with the following criteria for suicide:

(a) **Age and Sex**. Suicidal threats made by men appear to be activated more frequently than are those made by women. The older the person, the higher the probability of suicidal intention. Both age and sex should be considered. A statement of suicidal intent from a woman over 40 years of age is usually more dangerous than one from a boy 10 years of age. Note, however, younger people do make attempts, even if the aim is to manipulate and control.

(b) **Mood**. If, on a "hot-line" the caller sounds tired, depressed, "washed out", then the suicidal risk is higher than if the caller seems to be in control of him or herself. Exuberance, flight of ideas, screaming and yelling are considered ominous signs. Strong denial of suicidal intention should be considered a definite danger signal. If the caller's mood undergoes marked change for the better during the conversation, this is an indication that the risk of suicide may have increased.

(c) **Prior Attempts or Threats**. Recent studies show that in about 75% of actual suicides, there have been previous attempts.

(d) **Acute or Chronic Situation**. Acute depression is usually a sign of greater immediate danger but has a better prognosis for improvement than does a chronic situation.

(e) **Means of Possible Self-destruction**. The most deadly means of suicide are shooting, hanging, and jumping. If the caller is threatening to use any of these methods, and the means are avail-

57

able you *must* consider the threat serious and the risk high. Other methods such as the use of drugs, carbon monoxide poisoning, or wrist slashing can be equally lethal and should not be discounted because they appear to be slower and less dangerous.

(f) **Specific Details of the Method**. When the caller has named the method he or she intends to use and gives details about the time and place, the caller should be considered to be in danger.

(g) **Recent Loss or Separation From a Loved One**. When death of a loved one and/or divorce and separation are part of the picture, the danger of suicide increases. Even when separation has not already occurred, the person may feel deeply depressed. If there is any actual or impending loss of a loved one, suicidal danger increases.

(h) **Medical Symptoms**. If such facts as unsuccessful surgery, chronic debilitation, cancer or fear of cancer, asthma, fatigue, impotence, loss of sexual desire or any medical symptom come into the picture, the risk of suicide increases. This is especially true in older persons who may fear never regaining their health. Elderly people are sometimes plagued by feelings of loneliness and abandonment which cause them to exaggerate their physical ailments.

(i) **Diagnostic Impressions**. Making a psychiatric diagnosis is a professional task; however, the counselor should record symptoms so that a professional evaluation can be made later. Obvious signs such as hallucination, delusion, loss of contact with reality, will reveal a disoriented state. If such states as depression, anxiety, alcoholism, and homosexuality enter into the picture then the danger of suicide increases.

(j) **Resources**. If the caller is under financial stress, or has no friends or is all alone and has few or no social contacts, then the suicidal danger increases.

(k) **Living Arrangements**. The greater the satisfaction of the client in the area, the lower the risk. Four questions are useful:

   (1) Who is (are) the person(s) the client is living with at the present time?
   (2) What is the quality and quantity of their relationships?
   (3) Is the client satisfied?
   (4) Are these arrangements economically, emotionally, and socially adequate and supportive for the client at the present time? Callers who live alone, have few friends or other support systems or are unhappy in their living arrangements are great risks.

(l) **The Client's Perceptions of His or Her Problem**. Clients who feel that their situation is hopeless or that they are helpless to deal with the problem are greater risks.

(m) **Disruption of Daily Living Patterns**. The client who is out going to work, who is not eating well, who has lost weight and who is not able to carry on daily routine is a higher risk than one who is not so affected.

(n) **Coping Strategies and Devices**. How has the client dealt with crises in the past? How well did his or her strategies work? Is the client impulsive? Does the client habitually use excessive drinking, drugs or violent behaviors to cope with feelings about himself/herself or others?

B. *Treatment Phase*

The counselor should have a medical doctor to whom he can refer.

**Step #1:** The counselor should be aware of the steps to take in working with and assessing potential suicides.

**Step #2:** The counselor should remain composed during the session in which the threat occurs. The counselor should not become distressed or excited by the threat.

**Step #3:** The counselor should listen to what the client is saying, ask questions to determine the intensity of the threat, and review the threat with a referral resource physician.

**Step #4:** Prior to leaving the session, the counselor should discuss the situation with his or her supervisor or administrator. The supervisor can then help the counselor determine if there is a need for immediate specific action beyond that of contacting the referral resource physician. (a) The counselor should continue the session until it is felt that the danger of suicide is no longer present. (b) The counselor should enter into a "No-Suicide Contract" with the client and agree to immediate referral to a resource physician.

**Step #5:** Upon completion of the session, the counselor, administrator and supervisor (if one is available), should review the session and determine what specific action is appropriate. This might include notifying other professional people and/or specific contact sources such as the police, parents, relatives and/or ministers.

**NOTE:** The counselor should also note that according to the Tarasoff case, *Tarasoff vs. UC Regents*, (1974) . . . "protective privilege ends where public peril begins." What that means is that when there is danger to the person's life (suicide) or to the life of another (homicide), or to property, the psychotherapist (counselor) has a legal obligation to warn relatives (as in the case of intended suicide) or intended victims (as in the case of intended homicide). This could mean contacting parents, guardians, security officers, school administrators, and/or the person's medical doctor (see Principle #5 — Confidentiality — in Section IV, Ethics and Issues; also see Section III, Subsection B, Counseling Services Intake Form).

**NOTE:** Counselors should prepare for such an emergency by discussing the potential threat of suicide with those professional people who might be involved in immediate referral and treatment.

III. **Sources of Further Information**:

For further information see:

Forrest, D. V. (1983). Depression: Information and intervention for school counselors. *The School Counselor, 30,* 269-279.

Hatton, C. L., Valente, S. M., & Rink, A. (Eds). (1977). *Suicide: Assessment and intervention.* New York: Appleton-Century-Crofts.

Lerman, C. A., & Baron, A., Jr. (1981). Depression management training: A structured group approach. *The Personnel and Guidance Journal, 60,* 86-88.

McBrien, R. J. (1981). Coaching clients to manage depression. *The Personnel and Guidance Journal, 59,* 429-432.

Morgan, L. B. (1981). The counselor's role in suicide prevention. *The Personnel and Guidance Journal, 59,* 284-286.

Wekstein, L. (1979). *Handbook of suicidology: Principles, problems and practice.* New York: Brunner/Mazel.

# OBSESSIVE-COMPULSIVE BEHAVIOR

## I. Description

Obsessive-compulsive behavior is a situation in which a person becomes obsessed with an idea and feels compelled to respond to it in a certain way. It is characterized by overpowering feelings, thoughts or pressures to think or behave in ritualized ways. The persistent feelings are called obsessions; the expressed behavioral acts are referred to as compulsions.

Obsessive-compulsive behavior refers to thoughts, feelings, ideas and impulses that an individual cannot dispel in spite of an inner desire to do so. The compelling nature of the activity, even though it may be illogical, undesirable, and unnecessary, is the central issue. Generally such thoughts or feelings are alien to the individual's usual attitudes and are experienced as being disgusting, and at times, frightening. Their presence is sometimes embarassing and sometimes disturbing. It is an intriguing development, particularly in the face of current notions of free will and freedom of choice, because despite all the wishes, desires, and active opposition, the person is forced by some internal pressure to process cognitively a variety of experiences that may be distasteful or frightening. The distress can be severe enough to immobilize the individual and impair his or her functioning.

## II. Treatment Procedure

### A. *Assessment Phase*

Assessment of obsessive-compulsive behavior is not easily done through the use of standardized tests. Observation of a person will, however, reveal the following characteristics:

The obsessive-compulsive person has tendency to

(a) move against others
(b) be overly meticulous and perfectionistic
(c) fear failure and rejection
(d) attack and criticize others
(e) project to others (especially by blaming others)
(f) attempt to gain complete control of any situation he or she is in .

### B. *Treatment Phase*

The following steps are involved in the treatment phase:

**Step #1:** The person might try negative practice. That is, the person can use a satiation technique, i.e. the use of repetitive thought, image or impulse, to neutralize the obsessive-compulsive urge.

**Step #2:** The counselor might also try a cognitive approach by helping the person develop counter thoughts or images that reduce the discomfort caused by the obsession. Generally, a compulsive checking ritual is viewed as a repetitive attempt to gain reassurance.

**NOTE:** Other techniques such as flooding, imagery, and thought stopping have been used in dealing with obsessive-compulsive behavior, but only with limited success. It has often proved necessary to supplement these techniques with insight oriented therapy in order to deal effectively with the stress accompanying rituals and obsessions.

## III. Sources of Further Information:

For additional information read:

Rachman, S. (1976). The modification of obsessions: A new formulation. *Behaviour Research and Therapy, 14*, 437-443.

Rachman, S., & De Silva, P. (1978). Abnormal and normal obsessions. *Behaviour Research and Therapy, 16*, 233-248.

Salzman, L. (1980). *Treatment of the obsessive personality*. New York: Jason Aronson.

## SECTION III

## FORMS, CONTRACTS, AND LETTERS

### A FLOW CHART ILLUSTRATING CLIENT TREATMENT

THE forms and contracts which follow are preceded by a flow chart which illustrates the sequence of steps by which treatment can be initiated and pursued. Modifications can be made whenever it seems in the best interests of your own counseling program. It should be noted that these forms and contracts are a means of gaining direction. A careful study of this material may help the counselor to understand what steps can be taken to insure the ethical treatment of clients as they move through treatment services.

When reviewing the Intake Forms, please note that the Intake Forms have been presented in terms of the information that is most essential to the particular services. This provides the counselor with the opportunity to build a broader and more comprehensive data base from which to work.

Please Note: *All forms* and *contracts* should be modified to comply with State and Federal regulations. This means that all forms and contracts should be reviewed whenever State and Federal health and social welfare regulations are changed. It is the responsibility of the counselor to remain current regarding such legislation.

# A FLOW CHART ILLUSTRATING CLIENT TREATMENT

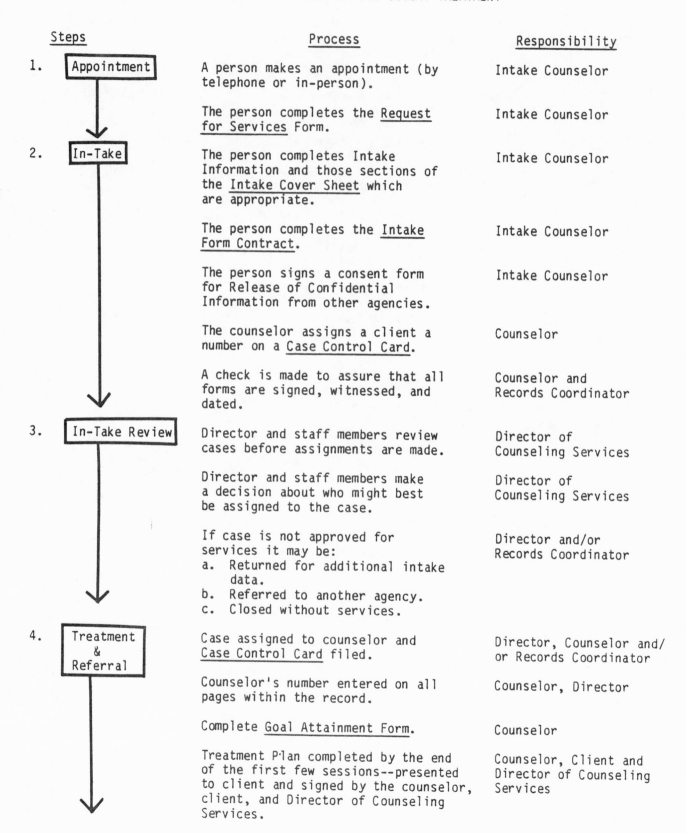

| Steps | Process | Responsibility |
|---|---|---|
| 1. Appointment | A person makes an appointment (by telephone or in-person). | Intake Counselor |
|  | The person completes the Request for Services Form. | Intake Counselor |
| 2. In-Take | The person completes Intake Information and those sections of the Intake Cover Sheet which are appropriate. | Intake Counselor |
|  | The person completes the Intake Form Contract. | Intake Counselor |
|  | The person signs a consent form for Release of Confidential Information from other agencies. | Intake Counselor |
|  | The counselor assigns a client a number on a Case Control Card. | Counselor |
|  | A check is made to assure that all forms are signed, witnessed, and dated. | Counselor and Records Coordinator |
| 3. In-Take Review | Director and staff members review cases before assignments are made. | Director of Counseling Services |
|  | Director and staff members make a decision about who might best be assigned to the case. | Director of Counseling Services |
|  | If case is not approved for services it may be:<br>a. Returned for additional intake data.<br>b. Referred to another agency.<br>c. Closed without services. | Director and/or Records Coordinator |
| 4. Treatment & Referral | Case assigned to counselor and Case Control Card filed. | Director, Counselor and/or Records Coordinator |
|  | Counselor's number entered on all pages within the record. | Counselor, Director |
|  | Complete Goal Attainment Form. | Counselor |
|  | Treatment Plan completed by the end of the first few sessions--presented to client and signed by the counselor, client, and Director of Counseling Services. | Counselor, Client and Director of Counseling Services |

65

| Steps | Process | Responsibility |
|---|---|---|
| 5. Quality Control | Complete the Quality Assurance Checklist at the end of the 3rd week, at intervals of 3 weeks and at termination. | Director of Counseling Services |
| | Review with Counselor for non-compliance and for corrections. | Director and Counselor |
| | Complete the CASE SUMMARY. | Counselor |
| | Complete the Goal Attainment Form, this time with the client. | Counselor and Client |
| | "Case Staffing." Counselors should consider staffing cases with ethical or legal implications at the earliest possible convenience. Monitoring and staffing of cases should be ongoing at all times. | Counseling Staff |
| 6. Termination | Complete Exit Interview Rating Sheet. | Counselor and Client |
| | Review case summary:<br>a. Client Identification and Counselor Identification Number<br>b. Dates of sessions and summary of hours<br>c. Goals of therapy<br>d. Activities involved (Types of services)<br>e. Outcomes<br>f. Recommendations<br>g. Referrals | Counselor |
| | Referral. Complete Consent for Release of Confidential Information. | Counselor, Client, Director and Witness |
| | Complete the<br>a. Interview and Testing Record Form<br>b. Counseling Services Perpetual Inventory<br>c. Counseling Case Load Record<br>d. Group Experience Case Load Record | Counselor and Coordinator or Records |
| 7. Records | Forms for Yearly Reports<br>In preparation for reporting services, make sure the following are included:<br>a. Counseling services Interviewing and Testing Record<br>b. Counseling Services Perpetual Inventory<br>c. Counseling Case Load Record<br>d. Group Experience Case Load Record | |

## Subsection A

## REQUEST FOR SERVICES FORM

THIS section contains two request forms: (a) A request form for individual services, and (b) a form which can be used for couples or families requesting services. Request forms are an essential part of a counseling services center because they permit people to request services at their own personal convenience. Such forms also make it possible for the counseling services center to set up a special time for a formal intake interview.

# COUNSELING
## Request for Services Form
### (Individuals)

NAME:_____     DATE:_____

CLIENT'S NUMBER:_____     PHONE (home):_____

ADDRESS:_____        (business:_____

_____

Marital Status (check one):

    Single____ Married____ Divorced____ Separated____ Widowed____

Age:___    Sex:___    Date of Birth:_____

Referral Source:_____

_____

_____

Education:_____

_____

_____

Employment:_____

_____

_____

Family Members:_____

_____

_____

Previous or Present Counseling or Therapy:_____

_____

_____

****             ****             ****

I would like to request services for myself (my child).

_____          _____     _____
    Witness                          Signature                Date

Client (student) Number:_____        Case Number:_____

### Request for Services
### (Couples/Families)

DATE:_____

HUSBAND'S NAME:_____        WIFE'S NAME:_____

ADDRESS:        _____        PHONE:_____

_____

MARITAL STATUS:  Single_____  Married_____  Divorced_____  Separated_____

AGE:_____  SEX_____  DATE OF BIRTH_____  DATE OF MARRIAGE_____

REFERRAL SOURCE:_____

EDUCATION:_____

_____

EMPLOYMENT:_____

_____

FAMILY MEMBERS: (parents, siblings, dependents)_____

_____

_____

FAMILY PHYSICIAN:_____

PRESENTING CONCERN:_____

_____

**************************************************************************

I/We would like to request marriage/family counseling services.

_____        _____
Husband's Signature             Wife's Signature

_____        _____
Witness                         Date

## Subsection B

## INTAKE FORMS

THE process of doing intakes must be carefully documented. The reason for this is that in recent years, the law has mandated informed consent for services such as counseling. What this means is that the client or student who applies for counseling services has the "right" to know what services he or she will receive, how these services are to be carried out, and under what conditions the services will be rendered.

These forms were designed to provide both the counselor and the client with the information they need prior to the implementation of counseling services. The Intake Forms Cover Sheet is simply a check list to make sure that the counselor has not forgotten anything. The Intake Form Contract is to help clients or students understand the conditions upon which they are entering into the counseling relationship, how the information will be treated and how and under what circumstances information can or will be transmitted to other persons or agencies.

GENERAL RULES/CONSIDERATIONS FOR INTAKE INTERVIEW

1.  Develop a working familiarity with the intake form.

2.  Let the interview flow smoothly.

3.  Try to ask questions in an open-ended fashion--give the client a chance to speak freely.

4.  Try to move from general (open-ended) questions to more specific (less global) questions within a given topic area.

5.  Ask questions which will help the client to define his or her problem.

6.  Permit a limited catharsis, but remember that the intake interview is an information-gathering session.

7.  Permit positive expectancy about receiving help, but make it clear that the case will not be assigned until after it is staffed.

## COUNSELING SERVICES CENTER

## INTAKE FORMS COVER SHEET

Counselor #:_____                    Client #:_____

_____Request for Services (signed, witnessed and dated)

_____Intake Form (completed with Intake Counselor's signature and times
      which client is available)

_____Confidentiality Agreement Form (signed, witnessed and dated)

_____Release of Information Form (from other agencies to the Counseling
      Service, completed in two copies with appropriate signatures and
      dates.)


_____      _____
Signature, Intake Counselor            Date

Record is complete


_____      _____
Signature, Case Record Coordinator     Date

*********************************************************************************


## CASE ASSIGNMENT

_____Intake Approved for Assignment to Counseling Service Personnel____.


_____      _____
Signature, Director                    Date

_____Intake Returned to Case Record Coordinator for additional
      information.

Specific Comments:_____

_____


_____      _____
Signature, Director                    Date

_____Record-Intake Corrected and Returned to Director.


_____      _____
Signature, Case Record Coordinator          Date

Presenting Concern:_____

_____

_____

_____

Significant Past Events:_____

_____

_____

_____

_____

Expectations of Counseling:_____

_____

_____

_____

_____

<u>Mental Status</u>

Attitude and Manner:_____

_____

Mental Activity:_____

_____

Mood and Emotional Reactions:_____

_____

Mental Content:_____

_____

(To be explored as relevant to the client's problem)

Social History:

Family Relationships:_____

_____

Friends:_____

_____

Dating:_____

_____

Preferred Activities:_____

_____

Living Patterns:_____

_____

Educational/Vocational History:

Goals:_____

_____

Work/School Record:_____

_____

Current Level of Satisfaction:_____

_____

Areas of Concern:_____

_____

Medical History:

Major Present or Past Medical Problem:_____

_____

Current Physician/Medication:_____

_____

_____

<u>Impressions and Recommendations</u>:

Primary needs of client (student):_____

_____

_____

_____

Hypotheses Regarding Nature of client's (student's) problem:_____

_____

_____

_____

Areas for Further Exploration:_____

_____

_____

_____

Type of Counseling/Intervention Appropriate:_____

_____

_____

Personal Perceptions:_____

_____

_____

_____

_____

Recommendations for Counseling Services:_____

_____

_____

_____

_____

_____
Intake Interviewer's Signature

Hours Available: Mon._____ Tues._____ Wed._____ Thurs._____ Fri._____

## COUNSELING SERVICES INTAKE FORM (CONTRACT)

Counseling consists of professional services to individuals and families. The services encompass a range of normal and/or developmental concerns. Emphases are on the acquisition or improvement of environmental coping skills, the development and improvement of problem solving and decision making capabilities, the development of strategies for coping with pressure (conflict or frustration), the establishment (where necessary) of a plan of rehabilitation for reentry into society after debilitating illness or trauma, and the development of process orientation for entry into careers.

In using these services the client (student) and his/her parent or guardian, if appropriate, will request the services or grant permission for the services.

It should be clearly understood that the information obtained from or divulged by the client (student and his parents) is treated with the strictest confidence and that such information will not be transmitted to any person or agency except in the following instances:

1.  By prior written consent of the client (student) or in the case of a minor the consent of his/her parent or guardian.
2.  To medical personnel in the event of a bona fide medical emergency.
3.  To qualified personnel conducting research, management audits, financial audits or program evaluation, but client (student) identities may not be revealed directly or indirectly.
4.  By an appropriate court order of competent jurisdiction. This, however, will be granted only after application showing good cause and careful consideration of the need for disclosure as weighed against injury to the client, to the client/counselor relationship and/or to the program of counseling services.
5.  To institutional authorities in the event that the information revealed does, in the counselor's judgment, indicate clear and imminent danger to the client (student), another individual, or society. This would include, but would not be restricted to, statements alluding to suicide or homicide.

I have read the previous statement and understand its contents. I hereby agree to the following:

1.  Taping of counseling sessions, by authorized request, i.e. the signatures of the client and his/her parents if tape recordings are deemed necessary for the welfare of the client (student).
2.  That the counseling staff can, if deemed essential to the welfare of the client (student), listen to or view the tape to determine his or her progress as well as to review the counseling strategies used.
3.  That what is said or done by the client (student) will be kept in confidence and not be transmitted outside of the Counseling setting, except in those instances stated above.
4.  Testing, if it is deemed necessary by the client (student) and counselor for additional case information.
5.  The case records maintained concerning my counseling will be retained in a confidential file. They will be routinely destroyed after four years, with the identification card being destroyed after seven years, from the termination of counseling.

_____          _____
Witness's Signature                  Client's Signature


_____          _____
Date                                 Parent's Signature (if appropriate)

**Subsection C**

# THE DEVELOPMENT AND USE
# OF A CASE CONTROL CARD AND
# PROBLEM AREAS CODING SYSTEM

THE purpose of the control card is to maintain a file on all clients (students) admitted for counseling services. It can later be used as a cross reference file for other more detailed records kept by the counselor. Recent recommendations concerning the storage of confidential information indicates that the information should probably be stored for 7 years before it is destroyed. The Problem Areas Coding System helps the counselor to profile his or her client, to define baseline characteristics of the client, and to record changed behavior when it occurs.

CASE CONTROL CARD

```
┌─────────────────────────────────────────────┐
│  Client's Name:_____#_____      │
│                                              │
│  _____M F   Age:____     │
│                                              │
│  Date started:_____ Date Term:____      │
│                                              │
│  Type service:_____ Code_____        │
│                                              │
│  Referred by:_____       │
│                                              │
│  Release signed: yes no_____       │
│                                              │
│  Information sent:_____ Date:____        │
│                                              │
│  Referred to:_____ Date:_____        │
│                                              │
│  Counselor:_____#_____          │
└─────────────────────────────────────────────┘
```

Case Control Card Instructions

1)  A Case Control Card is a form that enables the counselor to keep track of the cases that are being or have been seen.

2)  After doing an intake, a control card can be filled out and forwarded to the assigned counselor.

3)  Upon receipt of the case folder, the case control card should be removed from the file. The counselor should complete:

    1) Counselor's name
    2) Counselor's number

4)  The counselor should note the case number and place the control card in the active case card file.

5)  Upon closing of the case the control card should be completed by the counselor and placed in the Inactive Case Control Card File. When closing a case, the case folder should be placed in an inactive records file where it should remain until destroyed or reactivated. The policy for maintaining inactive folders is not always mandated by the state in which the counselor is working. it is probably a good idea to establish a policy regarding the maintenance of inactive folders, how the information will be destroyed and how long it will be maintained before being destroyed. It is probably an equally good idea to mandate what testing materials will be valid after one year.

82       *The Counselor's Desk Manual*

Problem Areas Coding System

| ADULT/COLLEGE | | |
|---|---|---|
| Code | Description | Which Goals Relate to Which Problem Areas |
| 1-01 | Social Activities/Skills | |
| 1-02 | Assertiveness | |
| 1-03 | Alcohol/drugs | |
| 1-04 | Anxiety | |
| 1-05 | Decision-Making | |
| 1-06 | Dependency | |
| 1-07 | Depression | |
| 1-08 | Fears (Phobias) | |
| 1-09 | Interpersonal Relations | |
| 1-10 | Marriage/Family | |
| 1-11 | Medication/Treatment | |
| 1-12 | Obsessions/Compulsions | |
| 1-13 | Psychosis Indicators | |
| 1-14 | Self-Care Skills | |
| 1-15 | Sexual Problems | |
| 1-16 | Somatic Complaints | |
| 1-17 | Work Related | |
| 1-18 | Education Related | |
| 1-19 | Other | |

| CHILD | | |
|---|---|---|
| Code | Description | Which Goals Relate to Which Problem Areas |
| 2-01 | Academic Skills (Reading, Math) | |
| 2-02 | Motor Skills | |
| 2-03 | Language/Speech Skills | |
| 2-04 | Social Skills with Adults | |
| 2-05 | Social Skills with Peers | |
| 2-06 | Eating, Toileting, Sleeping Skills | |
| 2-07 | Classroom Behavior | |
| 2-08 | Behavior/Other Skills | |
| 2-09 | Other Self-Care Skills | |
| 2-10 | Regard for Property | |
| 2-11 | Sex-Role Behavior | |
| 2-12 | Sexual Problems | |
| 2-13 | Overcoming Fears | |
| 2-14 | Appropriate Behavior for Situations | |
| 2-15 | Decision-Making | |
| 2-16 | Education/Vocation Planning | |
| 2-17 | Alcohol/Drugs | |
| 2-18 | Other | |

TO BE COMPLETED AT THE END OF COUNSELING:

1. Disposition (Check One): Terminated____, Continued____, Referred____, Failed to Return____

2. Number of Appointments Kept: ____

## Subsection D

## INTAKE APPOINTMENTS, CLIENT LOG AND
## THE COUNSELOR'S APPOINTMENT BOOK

IT IS a good idea to systematize your Intake appointments so that those who work within the Counseling Services Center can schedule appointments in a well coordinated way. The Counselor's Appointment Book is an excellent way of recording the number of clients who have used counseling services and on what day they were scheduled. This helps the administration to determine the days and hours of greatest flow.

The Client Log, on the other hand, provides the counselor with a perpetual inventory of all clients who have received services and the types of services received. It also provides the date when a case was terminated and how the disposition of the case was made.

INTAKE APPOINTMENTS - Week of: _____ to _____

| Hours | Monday | Tuesday | Wednesday | Thursday | Friday |
|---|---|---|---|---|---|
| 9 Cl: / Ph: / Co: | | | | | |
| 10 Cl: / Ph: / Co: | | | | | |
| 11 Cl: / Ph: / Co: | | | | | |
| COUNSELING SERVICES CENTER CLOSED FOR LUNCH | | | | | |
| 1 Cl: / Ph: / Co: | | | | | |
| 2 Cl: / Ph: / Co: | | | | | |
| 3 Cl: / Ph: / Co: | | | | | |
| 4 Cl: / Ph: / Co: | | | | | |

Cl = Client's name    Ph = Client's phone number    Co = Counselor's name

☒  Check if intake appointment is completed.

*The Counselor's Desk Manual*

COUNSELING SERVICES CENTER

CLIENT LOG

| Case Number | Client's Name | Co. Name & Number | Date of Assignment | Type of Services | Date Case Closed | Case Disposition |
|---|---|---|---|---|---|---|
| | | | | | | |
| | | | | | | |
| | | | | | | |
| | | | | | | |
| | | | | | | |
| | | | | | | |
| | | | | | | |
| | | | | | | |
| | | | | | | |
| | | | | | | |
| | | | | | | |
| | | | | | | |
| | | | | | | |
| | | | | | | |
| | | | | | | |
| | | | | | | |
| | | | | | | |

Counseling Services - Appointment Book - Week of _____

|  | Monday | Tuesday | Wednesday | Thursday | Friday |
|---|---|---|---|---|---|
| 8:00* | C1: _____ C2: _____ C3: _____ C4: _____ C5: _____ GR: _____ | C1: _____ C2: _____ C3: _____ C4: _____ C5: _____ GR: _____ | C1: _____ C2: _____ C3: _____ C4: _____ C5: _____ GR: _____ | C1: _____ C2: _____ C3: _____ C4: _____ C5: _____ GR: _____ | C1: _____ C2: _____ C3: _____ C4: _____ C5: _____ GR: _____ |
| 9:00 | C1: _____ C2: _____ C3: _____ C4: _____ C5: _____ GR: _____ | C1: _____ C2: _____ C3: _____ C4: _____ C5: _____ GR: _____ | C1: _____ C2: _____ C3: _____ C4: _____ C5: _____ GR: _____ | C1: _____ C2: _____ C3: _____ C4: _____ C5: _____ GR: _____ | C1: _____ C2: _____ C3: _____ C4: _____ C5: _____ GR: _____ |
| 10:00 | C1: _____ C2: _____ C3: _____ C4: _____ C5: _____ GR: _____ | C1: _____ C2: _____ C3: _____ C4: _____ C5: _____ GR: _____ | C1: _____ C2: _____ C3: _____ C4: _____ C5: _____ GR: _____ | C1: _____ C2: _____ C3: _____ C4: _____ C5: _____ GR: _____ | C1: _____ C2: _____ C3: _____ C4: _____ C5: _____ GR: _____ |
| 11:00 | C1: _____ C2: _____ C3: _____ C4: _____ C5: _____ GR: _____ | C1: _____ C2: _____ C3: _____ C4: _____ C5: _____ GR: _____ | C1: _____ C2: _____ C3: _____ C4: _____ C5: _____ GR: _____ | C1: _____ C2: _____ C3: _____ C4: _____ C5: _____ GR: _____ | C1: _____ C2: _____ C3: _____ C4: _____ C5: _____ GR: _____ |

Lunch: 12:00 to 1:00

|  | Monday | Tuesday | Wednesday | Thursday | Friday |
|---|---|---|---|---|---|
| 1:00 | C1: _____ C2: _____ C3: _____ C4: _____ C5: _____ GR: _____ | C1: _____ C2: _____ C3: _____ C4: _____ C5: _____ GR: _____ | C1: _____ C2: _____ C3: _____ C4: _____ C5: _____ GR: _____ | C1: _____ C2: _____ C3: _____ C4: _____ C5: _____ GR: _____ | C1: _____ C2: _____ C3: _____ C4: _____ C5: _____ GR: _____ |
| 2:00 | C1: _____ C2: _____ C3: _____ C4: _____ C5: _____ GR: _____ | C1: _____ C2: _____ C3: _____ C4: _____ C5: _____ GR: _____ | C1: _____ C2: _____ C3: _____ C4: _____ C5: _____ GR: _____ | C1: _____ C2: _____ C3: _____ C4: _____ C5: _____ GR: _____ | C1: _____ C2: _____ C3: _____ C4: _____ C5: _____ GR: _____ |
| 3:00 | C1: _____ C2: _____ C3: _____ C4: _____ C5: _____ GR: _____ | C1: _____ C2: _____ C3: _____ C4: _____ C5: _____ GR: _____ | C1: _____ C2: _____ C3: _____ C4: _____ C5: _____ GR: _____ | C1: _____ C2: _____ C3: _____ C4: _____ C5: _____ GR: _____ | C1: _____ C2: _____ C3: _____ C4: _____ C5: _____ GR: _____ |
| 4:00 | C1: _____ C2: _____ C3: _____ C4: _____ C5: _____ GR: _____ | C1: _____ C2: _____ C3: _____ C4: _____ C5: _____ GR: _____ | C1: _____ C2: _____ C3: _____ C4: _____ C5: _____ GR: _____ | C1: _____ C2: _____ C3: _____ C4: _____ C5: _____ GR: _____ | C1: _____ C2: _____ C3: _____ C4: _____ C5: _____ GR: _____ |

C = Cubicle     1,2,3,4,5 = Cubicle number for room assignments     GR = Group Room

## Subsection E

## QUALITY ASSURANCE CHECKLIST

THE Quality Assurance checklist is to determine where the counselor-client relationship is at any given time. It serves as a perpetual inventory with regard to the progress of both the counselor and the client. It is a method of implementing and maintaining high standards for the Counseling Services Center.

Counselor #:_____                                    Client #:_____

Quality Assurance Checklist

Instructions: Check all items which apply to the case being reviewed.

A. Treatment Plan

\_\_\_\_\_1. includes a presenting problem, measurable goals, and treatment activities.

\_\_\_\_\_2. specifies overall service strategies and time tables.

\_\_\_\_\_3. specifies family involvement in case

\_\_\_\_\_4. includes an expressed willingness on the part of the family to support the client.

\_\_\_\_\_5. includes Progress Chart entries.

\_\_\_\_\_6. includes well defined goal and treatment orientations.

\_\_\_\_\_7. includes recorded documentation of improvement (if any).

\_\_\_\_\_8. includes alternative treatment plans defined in the event of poor improvement orientations.

\_\_\_\_\_9. includes treatment progess.

\_\_\_\_10. includes an appropriate length of treatment in terms of stated goals.

\_\_\_\_11. includes evidence that the case has been staffed.

B. Referral Issues

\_\_\_\_\_1. All referrals made were appropriate.

\_\_\_\_\_2. The appropriate release forms are signed and dated.

\_\_\_\_\_3. Evidence of smooth intra-clinic referral or transfer (continuity of care) is indicated.

B. Referral Issues (continued)

\_\_\_\_\_4. When intra-clinic referral was made, there was adequate feedback given to the center.

\_\_\_\_\_5. There is evidence of a smooth transition outside of the center.

\_\_\_\_\_6. Recommendations for aftercare were given.

\_\_\_\_\_7. Appropriate referrals were made or considered.

C. Client's Rights

\_\_\_\_\_1. Client participated in treatment decision, including termination.

\_\_\_\_\_2. Client's confidentiality has been maintained (signed release for every outside contact).

\_\_\_\_\_3. Indications of rapport existed between client and therapist.

E. Testing (if appropriate)

\_\_\_\_\_1. The tests selected were appropriate to goals established.

\_\_\_\_\_2. If a testing report has been released to the client or to an agency, this has been documented.

\_\_\_\_\_3. Testing was appropriate in terms of the therapist's demonstrated competencies.

\_\_\_\_\_4. Tests were scored appropriately.

\_\_\_\_\_5. Test results were integrated into summary notes of therapy.

CO#_____                                                    CL#:_____

F.  Discharge and Termination

_____1. There is a discharge summary.

        2. The summary contains:

            _____a. the presenting problem

            _____b. course of treatment

            _____c. dispositon of the case

            _____d. assessment of treatment plan goals and objectives

            _____e. discharge instructions given to client

            _____f. recommendations for future treatment

_____3. Evidence of follow-up referral source.

                            Reviewed by:_____
                            Date:_____

Corrective Action Taken by Therapist:

_____

_____

_____

_____

_____

_____

_____

_____


_____        _____
Therapist                              Certified by Supervisor (Must be completed
                                       within one (1) week of receipt).

_____
Date

## Subsection F

## EXIT INTERVIEW RATING SHEET

ONCE the services of the counselor have reached a point where both the client and counselor agree to terminate, it is in the best interests of the Counseling Services Center to gather data regarding consumer satisfaction. That is, the Counseling Center will enjoy a better reputation if the counselors within that Center understand whether or not their clients were satisfied with the services offered. Such information will also help the counselors to render a service which is defensible during periods when budget cuts seem imminent.

# EXIT INTERVIEW RATING SHEET

Counselor's #:_____          Client's #:_____

CONSUMER SATISFACTION QUESTIONS:

1.  How satisfied were you with the services you received?

| Not at all Satisfied | Not very Satisfied | Somewhat Satisfied | Satisfied | Very Satisfied |
|---|---|---|---|---|

2.  Do you feel differently now about the concerns which led you to come for counseling services?

| Not at all Satisfied | Not very Satisfied | Somewhat Satisfied | Satisfied | Very Satisfied |
|---|---|---|---|---|

3.  Do you attribute this change in feeling (or lack of change) to the services you received here?

| No | Unsure | Yes |
|---|---|---|

4.  How do you feel about your progress?

| Not at all Satisfied | Not very Satisfied | Somewhat Satisfied | Satisfied | Very Satisfied |
|---|---|---|---|---|

GOALS SET FOR COUNSELING:

Goal #1

| No Progress | Little Progress | Some Progress | Good Progress | Very Good Progress |
|---|---|---|---|---|

Goal #2

| No Progress | Little Progress | Some Progress | Good Progress | Very Good Progress |
|---|---|---|---|---|

Goal #3

| No Progress | Little Progress | Some Progress | Good Progress | Very Good Progress |
|---|---|---|---|---|

95

## Subsection G

## CASE SUMMARY AND
## GOAL ATTAINMENT FORMS

THE Case Summary is exactly what is purports to be: a summary of the case stipulating the stated goals of the therapist and client, the evaluation of the extent to which those goals were met and whatever other comments seem appropriate to the case.

The Goal Attainment Form spells out, in detail, the stated goals of the client and the levels at which those goals were achieved, i.e. the extent to which the goals were met.

COUNSELING SERVICES CENTER

Counselor #:_____                    Client #:_____

CASE SUMMARY

Date of Intake:_____        Date of Termination:_____

Referred from:_____         Referral:_____

Referred to:_____           Continuation:_____

                                     Release date:_____

Number of Sessions:_____        Number of Hours:_____

GOALS OF THERAPY:

I.   _____Code:_____

     _____Level:_____

II.  _____Code:_____

     _____Level:_____

III. _____Code:_____

     _____Level:_____

                (attach additional sheets, if needed)

ACTIVITIES:_____

_____

_____

_____

EVALUATION: (as of_____date)_____

_____

_____

_____

Counselor #_____                    Client #_____

CASE SUMMARY (page 2)

RECOMMENDATIONS:

_____

OTHER COMMENTS:

_____

_____
Counselor's Signature

Release Approved:

_____
Director's Signature

GOAL ATTAINMENT FORM

Client No. _____   Treatment:   Ind: _____

Counselor No. _____   Group: _____

Session No. _____   Date: _____   Family: _____

| LEVELS OF OUTCOME | GOAL I | GOAL II | GOAL III |
|---|---|---|---|
| | I | LEVELS OF ATTAINMENT II | III |
| LEVEL A<br><br>Best anticipated success, i.e. Idealistic Improvement | | | |
| LEVEL B<br><br>Expected level of treatment success, i.e., realistic level of improvement | | | |
| LEVEL C<br><br>Most unfavorable outcome thought likely, i.e. no gain, or loss in functioning | | | |

NOTE: When you reach a point at which you plan to terminate with the client, have the client help you to evaluate your progress by checking the level you both agree you attained for each of the Goals. For purpose of rating, place a ( ✗ ) mark in the small box located in the square of each level of attainment.

_____
Signature, Counselor

_____
Date

_____
Client Signature

## Subsection H

## CONSENT FOR RELEASE OF
## CONFIDENTIAL INFORMATION

INFORMATION about the client cannot be released in many states without a formal consent for the release of such confidential information. The *Consent Release Form* serves as a format by which the counselor can design his or her own Release Form. Once developed, check with your licensure or certification board to make sure that your Release Form meets all the requirements of your state and that you are pursuing a sequence of steps which are both ethical and legal according to your state law.

COUNSELING SERVICES CENTER

Consent for the Release of

Confidential Information

I, _____of _____
        (name of client or participant)                              (client's address)

authorize_____to disclose to_____
        (name of agency making the disclosure)

_____
        (name of person or organization to which disclosure is to be made)

_____
                            (nature of information)

_____
                            (purpose of information)

    I understand that my records are protected under the Federal and State Regulations and cannot be disclosed without my written consent unless otherwise provided for in the regulations.  I also understand that I may revoke this consent at any time and that the request for revocation will be signed, dated and witnessed so that it does not conflict with requests made previously for release.

    Specification of the date, event, or condition upon which this consent expires:

_____

_____

    I further acknowledge that the information to be released was fully explained to me and this consent is given of my own free will.

    Executed this _____day of _____, 19____.


_____          _____
Witness                                 Signature of Client or Student

Please mail to: (Name and address
of Director of Counseling Services)     _____
                                        Signature of Parent (if appropriate)

                                        _____
                                        Signature of Authorized Program Rep.

## Subsection I

## FORMS FOR YEARLY REPORTS

THE Interview and Testing Record Form serves as an inventory report to the administration at the end of the year. It serves to help the administration understand how many people used your counseling services and for what purpose.

The Perpetual Inventory Form details the code number of clients served by any one specific counselor and the specific services rendered.

The Counseling Case Load Record Forms and the Marriage and Family Case Load Record Forms are inventories of group and family services rendered by the Counseling Services Center.

COUNSELING SERVICES CENTER INTERVIEW AND TESTING RECORD

COUNSELOR #_____

CLIENT #_____

NUMBER OF CONTACTS_____

NUMBER OF TESTS ADMINISTERED_____

NUMBER OF HOURS SPENT IN INTERACTION_____

NUMBER OF HOURS SPENT TESTING_____

NUMBER OF HOURS STAFFING_____

NUMBER OF HOURS CASE PREPARATION_____

TOTAL NUMBER OF HOURS OF CASE WORK_____

DISPOSITION OF CASE_____

TERMINATED: (Date:_____)

REFERRED TO:_____

CONTINUED:_____

PURPOSE OF COUNSELING:_____CODE:_____

(End of year report to the Administration)

COUNSELOR'S #: _____

Director's Name: _____

Period of Time Covered: _____

| Client's # | # of Contacts | # of Tests | Hours of Interact. | Hours of Testing | Hours Staff | Hours Prep. | Total Hours | Case Disposition | Counseling Code |
|---|---|---|---|---|---|---|---|---|---|
|  |  |  |  |  |  |  |  |  |  |
|  |  |  |  |  |  |  |  |  |  |
|  |  |  |  |  |  |  |  |  |  |
|  |  |  |  |  |  |  |  |  |  |
|  |  |  |  |  |  |  |  |  |  |
|  |  |  |  |  |  |  |  |  |  |
|  |  |  |  |  |  |  |  |  |  |
|  |  |  |  |  |  |  |  |  |  |
|  |  |  |  |  |  |  |  |  |  |
|  |  |  |  |  |  |  |  |  |  |
| TOTALS |  |  |  |  |  |  |  |  |  |

COUNSELING CASE LOAD RECORD

| CLIENT # | # of Con-tacts | # of Tests | Hrs. of Test. | Hrs. of Inter-action | Hrs. of Staff. | Hrs. of Prep. | Total Hours | Director's Initials | Date Intake / Date Term. | Disposition of Case | Counseling Code # |
|---|---|---|---|---|---|---|---|---|---|---|---|
| | | | | | | | | | | | |

## GROUP EXPERIENCE CASE LOAD RECORD

| CLIENT # | # OF SESSIONS | # OF HOURS | TYPE OF GROUP | SUPERVISOR | COMMENTS |
|---|---|---|---|---|---|
| | | | | | |
| | | | | | |
| | | | | | |
| | | | | | |

## MARRIAGE AND FAMILY CASE LOAD RECORD

| CLIENT # | # OF SESSIONS | # OF HOURS | TYPE OF GROUP | SUPERVISOR | COMMENTS |
|---|---|---|---|---|---|
| | | | | | |
| | | | | | |
| | | | | | |
| | | | | | |

OTHER COMPETENCIES: _____

## Subsection J

## TAPING YOUR COUNSELING SESSIONS

THE taping of counseling sessions is nothing new. Carl Rogers (1942) introduced the idea many years ago. The advantage of taping, however, is seldom discussed as a tool in counseling. Perhaps this is because so many training centers have accepted the necessity of it as a training technique that they have failed to recognize its absence in the school setting. Yet, many school counselors never tape.

The advantages of taping for school counselors appear to be threefold:

(a) Taping protects both the counselor and the client or student because the tape serves as a viable means of recapturing what occurred during any given counseling session.

(b) Taped sessions can be used for staffing and thus permit professional observations by other counselors. In this respect taped sessions provide a service which is in the best treatment efforts of the counselor.

(c) Taped sessions can be used in research studies to determine how students are responding to specific counselors and/or the techniques used by those counselors.

Before taping* any counseling session, it must be remembered that you cannot tape a counseling session without informed consent (the client must agree, by contract, that he or she will permit taping and must also agree to the purpose for taping). If the client is a minor (according to state law), then it will also be necessary to gain the consent of the parents or guardian.

**NOTE:** The counseling Intake Form (contract) includes permission to tape counseling sessions (See Section III, Subsection B).

---

Rogers, C. (1942). Electrically recorded interviews in improving psychotherapeutic techniques. *American Journal of Orthopsychiatry, 12*, 429-435.

Instructions for the Taping of Counseling Sessions

```
┌─────────────────────────────────────────────────┐
│              TAPE REQUEST FORM                   │
│                                                  │
│  CUBICLE NO:_____ TIME:_____   │
│                                                  │
│  AUDIO OR VIDEO:_____ DATE:_____   │
│                                                  │
│  TO BE MONITORED:_____ NOT MONITORED:____    │
│                                                  │
│  SUPERVISOR:_____   │
│                                                  │
│  NAME:_____ #_____   │
│                                                  │
│  CLIENT #:_____   │
│                                                  │
└─────────────────────────────────────────────────┘
```

1.  When possible, Counseling sessions should be taped.

2.  Before taping, counselors should complete a tape request form. These forms should be kept in the records office.

3.  When doing an intake the counselor should get the Consent for Services Form signed before taping. When this form is signed taping may begin.

4.  After finishing the taping session the tape should be filed in the records office or an area restricted to the use of counselors.

*NOTE:Before taping can be implemented, the Counseling Services Center Intake Form (contract) must be signed (see Section III, Subsection B).

## CASE MONITORING AND STAFFING

Director's initials and date when case was monitored by AV-TV or staffed:

|  | Date | Initials | Date | Initials | Date | Initials |
|---|---|---|---|---|---|---|
| Monitored: | _____ | , _____ | _____ | , _____ | _____ | , _____ |
|  | _____ | , _____ | _____ | , _____ | _____ | , _____ |
|  | _____ | , _____ | _____ | , _____ | _____ | , _____ |
|  | _____ | , _____ | _____ | , _____ | _____ | , _____ |
| Staffed: | _____ | , _____ | _____ | , _____ | _____ | , _____ |
|  | _____ | , _____ | _____ | , _____ | _____ | , _____ |
|  | _____ | , _____ | _____ | , _____ | _____ | , _____ |
|  | _____ | , _____ | _____ | , _____ | _____ | , _____ |

Supervisor's Comments about this case:

_____

_____

_____

_____

_____

_____          _____
Director's Signature                    Date

## Subsection K

# COUNSELING SERVICES CENTER GUIDELINES
# FOR CASE STAFFING

1. *Identifying Information*: Name (first name only), age, sex, referral source, mental status observation.

2. *Presenting Problem*: Client's description of the problem. Why is the client here for counseling?

3. *Background Information*: Information relevant to the presenting problem and including present circumstances.

4. Treatment Plan:

   A. *Assessment*: The Counselor' definition of the problem based on information obtained during counseling sessions and through the use of specific assessment techniques and instruments.

   B. *Treatment Goals*: These short-range and long-range goals stated in terms of expected and ideal levels of outcome. They answer the question, "How will the client change for the better?"

   C. *Literature Search*: An exploration of the literature to determine what research has been done in the problem areas stated during counseling sessions and what the researchers recommend for intervention strategies relative to these problems.

   D. *Intervention*: The implementation of a specific plan for intervention, including steps to be followed and techniques and/or tests to be used.

   E. *Rationale*: The reason for following a specific theoretical orientation.

   F. *Consultation*: (if appropriate)

5. *Summary*: the expected length of treatment, present status of the case and prognosis.

## Subsection L

## THE DEVELOPMENT AND USE
## OF COMPUTER SERVICES

COMPUTERS are not used in all counseling centers. However, when they are used, they serve the counselor well. The computer bank, can supply a list of well researched articles which can be of help to the counselor in selecting protocols to use with specific disorders, defects, deficiencies or disabilities. For example, a counselor working with a depressed client can retrieve from the computer a printout of references to articles dealing with depression. Once the counselor has read these articles, he or she may proceed with the case on the basis of well researched information. This research information, in turn, serves as a corpus of knowledge upon which the counselor's treatment techniques are based and thus places the counselor on sound ground ethically. The Literature Search Codes will help the counselor to realize how to use a computer terminal.

WHEN A COMPUTER SERVICE IS AVAILABLE

PROCEDURE FOR INITIATING A LITERATURE SEARCH REQUEST

```
+-------------------------------------------------+
| LITERATURE SEARCH REQUEST FORM                  |
|                                                 |
| NAME_____   |
|                                                 |
| DATE_____   |
|                                                 |
| CODES (ONE TO FOUR PER REQUEST)                 |
|                                                 |
| CODE #1_____CODE #2_____             |
|                                                 |
| CODE #3_____CODE #4_____             |
|                                                 |
|                                                 |
| SYSID_____DATE_____              |
|                                                 |
| TIME_____BY_____              |
+-------------------------------------------------+
```

1. A listing of hundreds of problem oriented categories can be posted on a Computer Terminal for treatment reference.

2. Catalog your problems into specific areas.

3. Enter the appropriate codes on a literature search request form.

4. Attach the completed form to the Bulletin Board in the Computer Terminal Room.

5. The request will usually be processed by 5:00 p.m. of the following day.

6. The print-out will be placed in a box on the desk in the Computer Terminal Room.

## LITERATURE SEARCH REQUEST CODES

| | | | |
|---|---|---|---|
| Abortion | ABOR | Disulfiram Ethanol Reaction | DERX |
| Acrophobia | ACRO | Divorce | DIVO |
| Adherence | ADHE | Driving Fears | SOLO |
| Adolescent Behavior Management | ADOL | Drug Dependency | DRUG |
| Adult Foster Care | AFCX | Dysmorphophobia | DYSM |
| Aggression | AGGR | | |
| Agoraphobia | AGOR | Earlier Waking | EARL |
| Alcoholism | ALCO | Eczematous Dermatitis | ECZE |
| Anger | ANGE | Emotional Disturbed | EMOT |
| Anorexia Nervousa | ANOR | Encopresis | ENCO |
| Antabuse | DERX | Enuresis | ENUR |
| Anxiety | ANXI | Episodic Dyscontrol | EPIS |
| Appropriate Shopping Behavior | ASBX | Erect Sitting Control | EXCX |
| Assertiveness | ASSE | Ethics | ETHI |
| Asthma | ASTH | Exhibitionist | EXHI |
| Attentive Behavior | ATTE | Expressing Feelings | EXPR |
| Auditory Hallucinations | AUDI | Extramarital Sexual Permissiveness | ESPX |
| Autism | AUTI | | |
| | | Family Disorders | FAMI |
| Back Pain | LBPX | Fathering | FATH |
| Bereavement | BERE | Fears | FEAR |
| Biofeedback | BIOF | Fetishism | FETI |
| Body Contortions | BOCO | Foster Parents | FOST |
| Borlerline Personality | BORD | Full Cleanliness Training | FCTX |
| Brain Damage | BRAI | | |
| Bruxism | BRUX | Gambling | GAMB |
| Bulimic Anorexic | BULI | Gender Role Behaviors | GRBX |
| | | Geriatrics | GERI |
| Cancer | CANC | Goal Attainment Scaling | GASX |
| Cannabis | CANA | Grief | GRIE |
| Cardiovascular Disease | CARD | | |
| Child Abuse | CHAB | Hallucinations | HALL |
| Child Gender Disturbances | CGDX | Handicapped | HAND |
| Child Management Problems | CHIL | Headache | HEAD |
| Cigarette Smoking | CIGA | Homicide Obsessions | HOMI |
| Classroom Behavior | CLAS | Homosexuality | HOMO |
| Cohabitation | COHA | Hospitalization | HOSP |
| Colitis | COLI | Housekeeping Skills | HOUS |
| Communication | COMM | Hyperactive | HYPA |
| Contraceptive Counseling | CONC | Hypertension | HYPT |
| Control Drinking | CODR | Hysteria | HYST |
| Coprophagic | COPR | | |
| Cough | COUG | Impotence | IMPO |
| Cramp | CRAM | Impulsive | IMPU |
| Crisis Intervention | CRIS | Inefficient Spending | INEF |
| | | Inhalent Abuse | INHA |
| Dating Anxiety | DATE | Insomnia | INSO |
| Death | DEAT | Instruction Following | INFO |
| Defensiveness | DEFE | | |
| Deindividualism | DEIN | Job Interview Skills | JISX |
| Delusional Behavior | DELU | Juvenile Delinquency | JUVE |
| Dental Fears | DENT | | |
| Depression | DEPR | Language Disorders | LANG |
| Deprivation | DEPV | Learned Helplessness | LEHE |
| Dermatosis | PSDE | Life Planning | LIFE |
| Developmental Problems | DEVE | Life Threatening Illness | LTIX |
| Diabetes | DIAB | Low Back Pain | LBPX |

| | | | |
|---|---|---|---|
| Manic | MANI | Sadism | SADI |
| Manic Depressive | MADE | Schizophrenia | SCHI |
| Mariguana | CANA | Seizures | SEIZ |
| Marital Problems | MAPO | Self Burning | SEBU |
| Masochism | MASO | Self Injurious Behavior | SIBX |
| Mastectomy | MASX | Self Talk (negative) | NSSX |
| Masturbation | MAST | Sex Role Behavior | SRBX |
| Memory Loss | MEMO | Sexual Abuse | SEAB |
| Menstrual Problems | MENS | Sexual Deviance | SEXD |
| Motion Sickness | MOTI | Sexual Dysfunction | SEXU |
| | | Sibling Conflict | SIBL |
| Nail Biting | NAIL | Sleep Disorder | SLEE |
| Nausea | NAUS | Snoring | SNOR |
| Negative Self-Statements | NSSX | Social Skill Deficit | SSTX |
| Neurologic Disorders | NEUR | Social Anxiety | SOAN |
| Neurosis | NEUX | Solo Driving | SOLO |
| | | Spasm | SPAS |
| Obesity | WEIG | Speech Anxiety | SPEE |
| Obsessional Thinking | OBTX | Spinal Chord Injury | SCIX |
| Obsessive-Compulsive | OBCO | Spouse Abuse | SPAB |
| Oncology | ONCO | Stealing | STEA |
| | | Stress Management | STCO |
| Pain | PAIN | Student Behavior | CLAS |
| Paranoia | PARA | Study Skills | STSK |
| Parenting Skills | PARE | Stuttering | STUT |
| Pedophillic Behavior | PEDO | Sucking Behavior | SUCK |
| Phenylketonura | PHEN | Suicide | SUIC |
| Phobia | PHOB | | |
| Phobic Dreams | PHDR | Tardive Dyskinesia | TARD |
| Physically Handicapped | PHHA | Tension | TENS |
| Pica | PICA | Test Anxiety | TEST |
| Pregnancy | PREG | Thumb Sucking | THSU |
| Premarital Sexual Intercourse | PSIX | Tics | TICS |
| Premature Ejaculation | PREM | Toilet Training | TOIL |
| Prenatal Influences | PREN | Tremor | TREM |
| Procrastination | PROC | Trichotillomania | TRIC |
| Professional Identity | PROF | | |
| Psychoses | PSYX | Unmotivated Patient Syndrome | UPSX |
| Psychosomatic Dermatosis | PSDE | Urination | URIN |
| Rape | RAPE | Vaginismus | VAGI |
| Remarriage | REMA | Vocational Indecision | VOCA |
| Renal Dialysis | REDI | Vomiting | VOMI |
| Retarded | RETA | | |
| Rocking | ROCK | Weight Control | WEIG |
| Ruminating Behavior | RUMI | Withdrawal | WITH |
| | | Women's Role | WOME |
| | | Work Adjustment | WORK |
| | | Writer's Cramp | WRIT |

## Subsection M

## REPORTING MAL-FUNCTIONING EQUIPMENT

IF you have equipment of any kind, i.e. overhead projectors, carousel slide projectors or video-taping equipment, you will immediately recognize the need for maintenance. This form was developed for counselors who can identify with this problem and who need to spend more time doing counseling and less time repairing their equipment. One should be careful to buy only those pieces of equipment on which their is a maintenance contract. If the company you plan to buy from does not supply a *good* maintenance contract, it is suggested that you shop around. By *good* is meant a contract which will be honored when the equipment needs repair. One way to determine the value of a maintenance contract is by going to former customers of the equipment company and checking the reputation of the company from whom you plan to buy. Another way to handle this is by having your chief administrator check on the company. A third approach is to read the contract carefully and then ask an attorney to read the contract and advise you on how to proceed. (The third approach may involve legal fees and should therefore be pursued only when you are ready to pay such fees.)

Reporting Mal-Functioning Equipment

MAL-FUNCTION REPORT FORM

```
┌──────────────────────────────────────────────────────────────┐
│                              Date:_____     │
│ Name of person filing report:_____│
│ Date of Mal-Function:_____Time:_____ │
│ Type of Equipment: VTR, ATR, Mike, Etc:_____ │
│ Equipment Number (if there is one):_____ │
│ Specification of problem:_____ │
└──────────────────────────────────────────────────────────────┘
```

A Mal-functioning report form should be filled out whenever a piece of equipment is not working properly. These forms should be available from the office of the coordinator of Counseling Services. Upon completion of the form, the person making the report should leave it with the director or coordinator of counseling services so that the equipment can be repaired as soon as possible.

## Subsection N

## SAMPLE LETTERS

Letters have to be designed with care both to avoid defamation and to insure constitutional rights. For example, the counselor cannot, without an appropriate release, disclose confidential information about a student. To do so, would violate the student's right to privacy.[1]* On the other hand, to release information which is basically incorrect, i.e. to breach the student's reputation, is to defame the student.[2]*

More simply put, what you say in a letter must be free of malice. For example, in the case of *Baskett vs. Crossfield*, 190 Ky 751, 228 SW 673 (1920)*, a university president informed the parents of one of his university students that their son had exposed himself (nude) at dormitory windows and was to be expelled for indecent exposure. The son responded by claiming that on several occasions he had simply forgotten to draw the blinds. The parents brought suit against the president.

The judgement by the court was that it was the duty of the president to report to the parents, that his letters were written in good faith, that there was no evidence of malice and that letters written in the line of duty, were privileged.

In another case, *Kenney vs. Gurley*, 208 Ala 623 95 S0 34 (1923)*, a dean wrote to a girl's parents that she had "not been living right" and should not return to school. The dean's letter was based on a medical report stating the girl had contracted a veneral disease.

The court held that the communication was privileged and that in the absence of malice, libel did not exist:

> Even if the diagnosis then made . . . was erroneous, or subsequently proved to be a mistake, that error of judgement . . . would not serve to afford evidence of actual or express malice.

After the *Thibadeau Case* (1960)* the New York Commissioner requested an opinion on the possible legal ramifications incurred by releasing records to parents. Counsel advised that:

> It is, therefore, my opinion that a carefully worded professional opinion rendered in line of duty by a physician, psychiatrist, psychologist, guidance counselor, principal or teacher, which is reasonably related to the educative process, made in good faith and with diligent regard for the rights of the person or persons involved is protected by a qualified privilege against civil actions for damages based on libel. Consequently, it would seem to me that such a law suit based on such a professional opinion against such persons would not be successful. *

---

[1] Prosser, Torts (1955) 572.
[2] Cooley, Torts (2d ed. 1888) 29.
[3] Themo vs. New England Newspaper Pub. Co. (Mass), 27 NE (2d) 753 (1940).
*NOTE: These cases can be found in Ware, M.L. (1964). *Law of guidance and counseling*. Cincinnati: The W. H. Anderson Company, pp. 43, 47, 117.
*Formal opinion of Counsel, No. 92. New York State Department of Education. November 17, 1960.

A Letter Designed to Encourage

Parents to Come in to Discuss Test Results

Re: Joe Smith: Age 18 - a senior at Central High School

Dear Mr. and Mrs. Smith:

We have completed our work with Joe and would like to discuss the results of the tests administered to him during the past few weeks. He has recently signed a release stipulating that we can discuss these results with you.

Should you care to pursue this matter further, please contact me at your convenience.

Sincerely Yours,


Letters Designed to Encourage

Parents to Come in to Discuss Personal Problems

A. Re: Mary Jones: Age 15 - pregnancy of which her parents are unaware

Dear Mr. and Mrs. Jones:

Mary has recently signed a Release of Information Form requesting that we talk with you regarding information which she has disclosed to us. She has also requested that she be present during the discussion and that she be permitted to introduce a personal management plan which she has worked out with the counseling staff.

Please contact me at your earliest convenience so that we can schedule an appointment.

Sincerely Yours,


B. Re: Jim Brown: Age 15 - recently caught in possession of drugs . .

. his parents are aware of the problem

Dear Mr. and Mrs. Brown:

We have recently talked with Jim and he has signed a Release of Information Form stipulating that the content of the information disclosed to us can be shared with you. It appears that such information might be of some value to you as you prepare to help Jim in his efforts to rehabilitate.

Sincerely Yours,

# SECTION IV

## ETHICS & ISSUES

ETHICS become extremely important to a manuscript of this nature because they serve as the standards by which counselors function. In essence, they detail for counselors descriptions of problematic situations in which other counselors have been involved. Thus, by reviewing court rulings and previous cases, counselors get a better impression of where they are going and how to get there while working in the best interests of their clients.

## Subsection A

## PROFESSIONAL ETHICS

INTERESTINGLY enough, we have two sets of ethical standards to which most counselors subscribe, i.e. those set forth by the American Association for Counseling and Development (AACD) (American Association for Counseling and Development, 1981)*, and those set forth by the American Psychological Association (APA) (American Psychological Association, 1967; 1981)†.

(a) Counselors subscribing to the Ethical Standards set forth by AACD would be bound by such concepts as the following:
   (1) Enhancing the worth, dignity, potential, and uniqueness of each individual
   (2) Improving one's professional practice
   (3) Behaving in an ethical way
   (4) Recognizing professional limitations
   (5) Establishing realistic professional fees
   (6) Pursuing ethical standards in counseling and testing individuals
   (7) Pursuing ethical standards in research and publication

(For a complete listing of the Ethical Standards of the American Association for Counseling and Development, see Appendix A).

(b) Counselors subscribing to the Ethical Standards set forth by APA would be bound by the following principles:
   (1) Responsibility
   (2) Competence
   (3) Moral and Legal Standards
   (4) Public Statements
   (5) Confidentiality
   (6) Welfare of the Consumer
   (7) Professional Relationships
   (8) Assessment Techniques
   (9) Research with Human Participants
   (10) Care and Use of Animals

(See complete listing of Psychological Ethical Standards in Appendix B).

Since the American Psychological Association has defined specific cases within the purview of its ethical standards, these ten ethical principles can be used to illustrate better how cases are reviewed and disposed of (American Psychological Association, 1967). Because of the objectivity attached to APA stan-

---

*Copyright AACD. Reprinted with permission. No further reproduction authorized without permission of AACD (See Appendix A).

†Copyright (1981) by the American Psychological Association. Reprinted/Adapted by permission of the publisher and author (See Appendix B).

dards by previous Committee review and court action, we have used these standards to explain the ethical position of counseling.

### Principle #1: Responsibility

Responsibility refers to the idea of maintaining "objectivity" and "integrity" while working with clients. It encourages the acceptance of responsibility for one's work which includes reporting results accurately. It also encourages counselors to avoid dual relationships which might interfere with objectivity, i.e. such things as the idea of dating clients or students while at the same time attempting to serve them as counselors. Finally, it suggests that counselors who are supervising others do periodic evaluations of these people and that these evaluations be both adequate and timely.

**Sample Problem #1**: You are a male counselor and one of your students (a female who is also your client) wants to go to the Christmas dance. Her boyfriend is suddenly called out of town and she asks you to take her. You are single, and like this girl vey much. How would you respond?

**Sample Problem #2**: A student transfers to another school and in so doing requests that his new counselor call you and request his records. How would you respond?

**Considerations:**

**Problem #1**: In sample problem #1, you would have to consider the responsibility of entering into a dual relationship which interferes with your objectivity. Such action creates an ethical breach.

**Problem #2**: In sample problem #2, to call or telephone without providing an appropriate request and signed release form would lack the objectivity necessary to remain ethical in transferring confidential information.

### Principle #2: Competence

Compentence refers to the skill with which you administer your counseling services. It not only includes your ability to understand your limitations, but your ability to remain current in your professional area. It also includes presenting material in a carefully prepared, accurate, current and scholarly manner. Finally, it mandates an understanding of measurement variables, validation problems and pertinent research before using test results for decision-making purposes.

**Sample Problem #1**: You have never given a Wechsler Intelligence Test before but one of your clients (a high school senior) needs a Wechsler test score immediately to be admitted to college. You have the test materials available in your office and have watched the test being administered on several occasions. No one else within a radius of 100 miles can administer the test. What would you do?

**Sample Problem #2**: A 16-year-old high school student comes into your office and reveals that she has recently been suffering from severe headaches. She claims that the headaches can start at any time and that the pain usually occurs near her temple and above her left ear. What would you do?

**Considerations:**

**Problem #1**: In problem #1, a counselor would place himself or herself in a position which was clearly unethical by testing with an instrument with which he or she had no expertise. To submit test scores based on such testing would simply compound the problem.

**Problem #2**: In problem #2, because of the nature of the complaint and the age of the student, the counselor should staff the case with the school nurse and the school administrator. Parents should then be contacted and the girl should be referred to a medical specialist who can most appropriately do further testing. In this case, that might be a neurologist (the choice of the neurologist to whom the client is referred should always rest with the parents or the client).

### *Principle #3: Moral and Legal Standards*

Moral and legal standards involve personal and professional conduct. They are guidelines by which the counselor attempts to avoid unjustifiable discrimination or activities which would violate or diminish another person's legal or civil rights. They are also guidelines which motivate the counselor to stay abreast of federal and state laws and to become familiar with regulations which govern his or her conduct while engaged in research or other activities with humans or animals.

**Sample Problem #1**: In the process of counseling, a 14-year-old female tells you she is considering suicide. What are your responsibilities relative to confidentiality and referral? How would you respond?

**Considerations:**

**Problem #1**: In the Tarasoff case (1974) a legal case which governs the answer to the problem, the judge ruled that ". . . protective privilege ends where public peril begins." What that means is that when a client reveals information indicating clear and imminent danger to oneself (as in suicide) or to another (as in homicide), the counselor is encouraged to reveal this information to institutional authorities and to the parents.

To avoid the difficulty normally involved in breaking confidentiality in situations like this, we suggest that you use a form similar to the Counseling Services Intake Form (see p. 78) to inform your client of the conditions under which a breach of confidence will be made. We would also suggest that you read these points to the client before beginning therapy to make sure that the client understands the conditions of the contracted counseling services.

## Principle #4: Public Statements

Public statements refer to misleading statements made by a counselor to imply personal qualifications, affiliations or sponsorships. This might include making false, fraudulent or deceptive statements; making laudatory claims for a technique or procedure; appealing to a person's fears; or soliciting people by claiming your services are better than the services of a competitor.

**Sample Problem #1**: As a counselor who specializes in reading problems, you advertise in the paper that you will guarantee that anyone who takes the course will be able to read 1,000 words per minute. You have several clients who are slow readers; their parents have the money for such a course. Is your statement ethical?

**Sample Problem #2**: You are asked to do a local television program in which you take problems submitted in writing from your viewing audience and respond to them by offering suggestions for coping with their difficulties. Is this practice ethical?

### Considerations:

**Problem #1**: In problem #1, it might be difficult to guarantee that any person taking the course would end up with the capability of reading 1,000 words per minutes. It seems therefore, that the statement might be fraudulent; it is certainly laudatory and therefore without taste. We feel that such statements are not in the best interests of the counselor nor of his or her profession.

**Problem #2**: In problem #2, it is difficult to believe that a counselor would even attempt to advise anyone on the basis of such limited information. At best, such advice would be questionable . . . at worst, it could be harmful. We feel that it is not in the best interests of counseling to become involved in such exercises.

## Principle #5: Confidentiality

Confidentiality refers to the handling of information received in confidence by the counselor. It also refers to how, and under what circumstances, if any, this information can be revealed to other people.

**Sample Problem #1**: (a) How do you handle demands by parents for tests results of their children? (b) How do you deal with records in the event of your counselor's death or disability?

**Legal Cases**: (a) Confidentiality of Records — Federal Privacy Act (PL 93-380) stipulates that school records are opened to parents whose children are in attendance and to those students who have reached the age of 18. The act applies to all schools receiving federal aid. All notes and reports prepared for release should be done with extreme care. (b) Holder of the Privilege — Check your state laws. States such as California (see California Evidence

Code 911-920 and 1010-1028) make it clear that it is the recipient of services (the client) who determines what may be released. (c) According to the *Tarasoff vs. U.C. Regents case* (California Supreme Court, 1974), protective privilege ends where public peril begins. What this means is that if the counselor has information indicating danger to the client's life (suicide) or should a client threaten harm to another person (homicide) or to property, this California Supreme Court ruling creates a guideline for counselors which indicates that it may be in their best interests to release information to appropriate sources.

## Considerations:

Nationally, there are varied opinions about this. Yet, it seems advisable that the counselor detail the conditions of his or her professional relationship with the client prior to serving that client. The Counseling Services Intake Form (See Section III, p. 78 — Forms & Contracts) is designed to do just that. This form helps to orient the client to the conditions of confidentiality.

### *Principle #6: Welfare of the Consumer*

Welfare of the consumer refers to standards of ethics which are provided in the best interests of the consumer. This includes avoiding sexual intimacies with you clients, defining financial arrangements for your clients before beginning services, defining the confidentiality of your services before implementing the services and helping your client to understand conflicts of interest, should such conflicts arise.

**Sample Problem #1**: One of the male counselors on your staff regularly sees a female client in his apartment after hours, and sometimes late at night. The counselor claims that this is necessary because there is no other time available. How would you respond to this?

**Sample Problem #2**: You are working as a counselor within the confines of a large public school setting. A young high school student walks in one day and requests counseling services. After listening to her story, you think that it might be in her best interests to be referred for biofeedback treatment. However, the girl is the daughter of the city superintendent of Public Schools. If you can help her, it may be important to your career. How would you respond?

## Considerations:

**Problem #1**: Before you can comment on the situation, the circumstances would have to be discussed with the counselor involved. Approaching your colleague and discussing the appearance of the situation might lead to a modification of his approach (See Principle #7). That is, he may modify the conditions of the case or, he may work out a more appropriate schedule with his client.

Problem #2: It is the counselor's responsibility to inform his/her client of the alternative treatment plan available and the potential value it has for her particular affliction.

### Principle #7: Professional Relations

Professional relations are those relations between the counselor and other professional colleagues. The principle stipulates that when working with others, each professional person is given appropriate credit for the work done; that each counselor maintain high standards of conduct by subscribing to the ethics of his or her profession; and that when referrals are made, the counselor have complete knowledge of the source to whom the client is referred.

**Sample Problem #1**: As a counselor, you have worked with problems related to obesity. Your work has been well received and you have been highly successful with your clients. However, to create the kind of climate absolutely necessary for safe weight reduction, you have used the services of a medical doctor who places all your obese clients on special diets. You have also used the services of a university exercise expert who has a degree in the physiology of exercise. Both the medical doctor and the exercise expert have contributed much to the success of your weight reduction program. Recently, a newspaper has requested that you do a series of articles related to your work. The first article is finished and it carries your name only. You have made no reference to the medical doctor nor to the exercise expert although some of the exercises and diets prescribed by these two people have appeared in your article. Have you acted in an ethical way?

**Considerations:**

**Problem #1**: To be ethical, you should include the names and contributions of those who have worked with you and contributed significantly to the writing, research and/or design of your study.

### Principle #8: Assessment Techniques

This principle refers to the construction and use of tests with clients. It makes imperative the idea that when tests are developed, they should conform to the Standards for Educational and Psychological Tests (APA, 1974); that when reporting results of standardized tests the interpretations are rounded and clear; that clients and their respective parents or guardians understand what information will be discussed; that all tests remain in tight security; that tests are used only in light of clearly formulated goals and hypotheses; that records of test results are not made available to those who do not need to see them; and that test results are released only after the client signs a release form. It is also important to inform clients that test results usually become less meaningful with age and that after one year tests should probably be retaken.

**Sample Problem #1**: As a counselor, you find that one of the teachers in your school has been going through the records of all of her students attempting to find I.Q. scores. Once she has these scores, she uses them as a basis for grading her students even though the I.Q. scores do not correlate well with the performance of her students on the tests she has developed for her course. What would you do?

**Considerations:**

**Problem #1**: Results of tests should not be released to those who do not need them. In this case, the teacher has no real need for this information. Second, the results of such information should be held in tight security. Obviously this has not been done. The counselor might consider moving this information into an area which is more secure. There should also be an attempt by the counselor to talk with the teacher and help her to understand that what she has done is not in the best interests of her students nor in the best interests of her profession.

### *Principle #9: Research with Human Subjects*

When doing research with human subjects, it is important for the counselor to inform the participant(s) of all features of the research that might be expected to influence his or her willingness to participate, e.g. providing the participant(s) with the option of having his or her data destroyed; providing the subjects with the freedom to participate in the research project or discontinue participation at any time; contracting with each participant in terms of an agreement which clarifies the responsibilities of the participant(s) and the counselor; taking all possible measures to minimize distress; and providing each participant with a signed copy of the contract.

**Sample Problem #1**: As a counselor and researcher you are conducting research which involves persuasion under conditions of ego-involvement and non-involvement, and includes some initial deception in terms of purported purposes of the research. You have failed to debrief your subjects and inform them of the deception following your collection of the data. What is the ethical thing to do?

**Considerations:**

**Problem #1**: Since subjects were not debriefed, one alternative you have is to give them the option of having their data destroyed. Preceding such an alternative and depending on the circumstances involved, you may want to provide the participants with a full clarification of the nature of the study prior to their decision to destroy the data. Any attempt to remove misconceptions might work in the best interests of saving the research.

## Subsection B

## PROFESSIONAL ISSUES

Issues about which counselors should know something:

### Issue #1: *Confidentiality of School Records*

Counselors should know that for schools receiving federal aid, the Federal Privacy Act (PL 93-380) made school records available to parents of school children and to students who had reached the age of 18. Since this privilege is not extended to all teachers, but only to those teachers who have a need for these records for instructional purposes, counselors must be discreet in processing confidential information about students and extremely careful in the preparation and release of materials concerning students.

### Issue #2: *The Holder of the Privilege*

When dealing with confidential information, it is the student or client about whom or for whom the information has been gathered who is the holder of the privilege. Thus, the student or client must determine what is to be released.

### Issue #3: *Who Holds the Privilege?*

Who holds the privilege, the child or the parent? State law sometimes makes the parents the holders of the privilege. To avoid conflicts about an issue such as this, the counselor should make sure that he or she has a contract with the parents stipulating the exact sequence of steps necessary for processing the child and the specific information to be transmitted to the parents as a result of treatment. The contract must be specific. Remember, if you are covered by insurance, that your insurance covers general damages. Releasing information without consent might fall into the category of punitive damages. Punitive damages are not normally covered by insurance policies. Releasing such information could serve as the basis for a lawsuit, especially when there is a willful disregard for someone's rights or safety. The counselor should also realize that confidential files when subpoenaed need only be presented in court. *It is important never to release information about a person unless you have a signed Informed Release Form from that person.* Our experience has been that the person's signature should be witnessed.

### Issue #4: *Sexual Intimacy (Assuming that both parties are of age and are capable of giving their consent)*

Although a sexual relationship between a counselor and a client or former client may not always be viewed as violating the law, it violates the ethical standards under which most counselors work, i.e. it is not a responsible act, it is not an act which is in the best interests or welfare of the client, it shows an insensitivity of community standards on the part of the counselor, and it places the counselor in a dual role (his/her emphasis is on self needs rather than client needs).

### Issue #5: Suicide or Homicide

The counselor should know and understand the implications of the *Tarasoff v. U.C. Regents case* (1974). The ruling in the case was that personal privilege ends where public peril begins. What that means is that if the counselor has information of a confidential nature which indicates that his or her client is about to inflict harm on someone else (homicide) or on himself or herself (suicide), the counselor has a legal obligation to warn the intended victim or those who might be expected to notify the person of the peril.

The Counseling Service's Intake Form (contract) in Section III, p. 78, is designed to help the counselor protect himself or herself against such an issue.

### Issue #6: Placement of Children in Special Education Classes

Counselors should know that Public Law 94-142, which went into effect in 1977, guarantees an appropriate free public education to all children who need special education services. The categories of classification differ from state to state but generally include such areas as the:

(a) Visually handicapped.
(b) Communication handicapped.
(c) Auditorially handicapped.
(d) Orthopedically handicapped.
(e) Emotionally disturbed.
(f) Mentally retarded.
(g) Neurologically impaired.

The key feature of Public Law 94-142 is that an *Individual Education Plan* (IEP) must be designed for each handicapped student. The IEP must be drafted by a committee of school personnel in collaboration with the parents of the handicapped child. The draft must include:

(a) A statement of the student's present level of academic performance.
(b) A statement of long range (annual goals) and short term goals.
(c) A statement of specific educational services to be provided and the extent to which the student will be able to participate in regular programs.
(d) The projected dates for implementing the services and their anticipated duration.
(e) Appropriate objective criteria for evaluation, the procedure by which evaluation will take place, and schedules for determining the extent to which educational objectives have been met.

**Important Classification Cases**

(a) *Mills v. Board of Education of the District of Columbia* (1972): Ruling — Free appropriate public education cannot be denied any retarded person aged 6 or more.

(b) *Diana v. California State Board of Education* (1973): Ruling — Restrained placement of Spanish speaking or bilingual children on the basis of an I.Q. test written in English in classes for the mentally retarded.

(c) *Larry P. v. Wilson Riles (Superintendent of the Board of Education, State of California)* (1972): Results — Placed an injunction on the use of standard I.Q. tests for placing black children in classes for the educable mentally retarded. There is some question about the definition and assessment of mental retardation, the validity of intelligence tests, and the effects of being placed in special education classes and labeled.

## *Issue #7: The Rights of Minors*

Counselors should know that the legal trend may be toward recognizing the personal rights of children as separate and distinct from the interests of their parents.

**Important Case**

*Porham v. JR and JL* (1976): Results — a three-judge federal court ruled that a Georgia state law which permitted the institutionalization of children by third parties (parents) without a court hearing violated the constitutional rights of the children.

## *Sources of Further Information:*

Corey, G., Corey, M. S., & Callanan, P. (1979). *Professional and ethical issues in counseling and psychotherapy*. Monterey, CA: Brooks/Cole.

Crawford, R. L., Murrell, D. S., & Murrell, P. H. (1981). Confidentiality of communications between juveniles and counselors. *AMHCA Journal, 3*, 22-26.

Denkowski, K. M., & Denkowski, G. C. (1982). Client-counselor confidentiality: An update of rationale, legal status, and implications. *The Personnel and Guidance Journal, 60*, 371-375.

Everstine, L., Everstine, D. S., Heymann, G. M., True, R. H., Frey, D. H., Johnson, H. G., & Seiden, R. H. (1980). Privacy and confidentiality in psychotherapy. *American Psychologist, 35*, 828-840.

Hare-Mustin, R. T., Marecek, J., Kaplan, A. G., & Liss-Levinson, N (1979). Rights of clients, responsibilities of therapists. *American Psychologist, 34*, 3-16.

Hendrickson, R. M. (1982). Counselor liability: Does the risk require insurance coverage? *The Personnel and Guidance Journal, 61*, 205-207.

Humes, C. W. (1982). Counselor role and responsibilities in special education heaings. *The School Counselor, 30*, 32-36.

Talbutt, L. C. (1983). Libel and slander: A potential problem for the 1980's. *The School Counselor, 30*, 164-168.

Van Hoose, W. H., & Kottler, J. A. (1977). *Ethical and legal issues in counseling and psychotherapy.* San Francisco: Jossey-Bass.

Wagner, C. A. (1981). Confidentiality and the school counselor. *The Personnel and Guidance Journal, 59*, 305-310.

# SECTION V

# TESTING: BUILDING A CONVENIENT
# TEST FILE

LOCATING tests when you need them is extremely critical to effective counseling. The most frustrating part of testing, however, is having a large library of tests and not knowing the grade levels or age levels covered by the tests. To provide the counselor with a quick overview of tests available and the grade and age levels for which they were designed, the revised GAT-SCAN*, i.e. the Gutsch-Alcorn Test Scanner (Gutsch & Alcorn, 1970) is included. The GAT-SCAN lists many of the tests presently used by counselors and provides (by virtue of the way it is organized) a method of filing tests for future use.

Code numbers on the GATS-SCAN can be translated to publisher's addresses by referring to The List of Test Publishers (pp. 155-157) and matching the code numbers with the publisher's numbers.

From the book, *Guidance In Action: Ideas and Innovations for School Counselors* by Kenneth U. Gutsch and John D. Alcorn © 1970, by Parker Publishing Company Incorporated, West Nyack, New York. Reprinted by permission of the publisher.

TEST FILING SYSTEM

GAT-SCAN

GRADE LEVEL

| TEST | CODE NO. | K | 1 | 2 | 3 | 4 | 5 | 6 | 7 | 8 | 9 | 10 | 11 | 12 | College | Adult |
|------|----------|---|---|---|---|---|---|---|---|---|---|----|----|----|---------|-------|
| **A. ACHIEVEMENT** | | | | | | | | | | | | | | | | |
| 1. Adult Basic Learning Examination | 24 | | | | | | | | | | | | | | | |
| 2. California Achievement Tests | 8 | | | | | | | | | | | | | | | |
| 3. Iowa High School Content Examination | 7 | | | | | | | | | | | | | | | |
| 4. Iowa Test of Educational Development | 29 | | | | | | | | | | | | | | | |
| 5. Iowa Tests of Basic Skills | 19 | | | | | | | | | | | | | | | |
| 6. Metropolitan Achievement Test | 24 | | | | | | | | | | | | | | | |
| 7. Sequential Tests of Educational Progress | 15 | | | | | | | | | | | | | | | |
| 8. SRA Achievement Series | 29 | | | | | | | | | | | | | | | |
| 9. Stanford Achievement Test | 24 | | | | | | | | | | | | | | | |
| 10. Test of Adult Basic Education | 8 | | | | | | | | | | | | | | | |
| 11. Wide Range Achievement Test | 17 | | | | | | | | | | | | | | | |
| **B. ACHIEVEMENT (DIAGNOSTIC)** | | | | | | | | | | | | | | | | |
| 1. Barrett Ryan English Test | 6 | | | | | | | | | | | | | | | |
| 2. Diagnosis: Mathematics | 29 | | | | | | | | | | | | | | | |
| 3. Diagnostic | 8 | | | | | | | | | | | | | | | |
| 4. Diagnosis: Reading Mathematics Inventory | 29 | | | | | | | | | | | | | | | |
| 5. Stanford Diagnostic Arithmetic Test | 18 | | | | | | | | | | | | | | | |
| 6. Woodcock Reading Mastery Test | 2 | | | | | | | | | | | | | | | |
| **C. ADJUSTMENT INVENTORIES** | | | | | | | | | | | | | | | | |
| 1. Adjustment Inventory | 11 | | | | | | | | | | | | | | | |
| 2. College Inventory of Academic Adjustment | 11 | | | | | | | | | | | | | | | |
| 3. Personal Adjustment Inventory | 4 | | | | | | | | | | | | | | | |
| **D. APTITUDE TESTS** | | | | | | | | | | | | | | | | |
| 1. Academic Promise Test | 24 | | | | | | | | | | | | | | | |
| 2. Aptitude Test for Occupations | 8 | | | | | | | | | | | | | | | |
| 3. Armed Services Vocational Aptitude | 3 | | | | | | | | | | | | | | | |
| 4. Detroit Test of Learning Aptitude | 5 | | | | | | | | | | | | | | | |

## TEST FILING SYSTEM

| TEST | CODE NO. | K | 1 | 2 | 3 | 4 | 5 | 6 | 7 | 8 | 9 | 10 | 11 | 12 | College | Adult |
|------|----------|---|---|---|---|---|---|---|---|---|---|----|----|----|---------|-------|
| **D. APTITUDE TESTS (cont.)** | | | | | | | | | | | | | | | | |
| 5. Differential Aptitude Test | 24 | | | | | | | | | | | | | | | |
| 6. Flanagan Aptitudes Classification Test | 29 | | | | | | | | | | | | | | | |
| 7. Flanagan Industrial Test | 29 | | | | | | | | | | | | | | | |
| 8. Macquarrie Test of Mechanical Ability | 8 | | | | | | | | | | | | | | | |
| 9. Minnesota Clerical Test | 24 | | | | | | | | | | | | | | | |
| 10. Multiple Aptitude Test | 8 | | | | | | | | | | | | | | | |
| 11. Revised Minnesota Paper Form Board Test | 24 | | | | | | | | | | | | | | | |
| 12. SRA Clerical Aptitude Test | 29 | | | | | | | | | | | | | | | |
| 13. SRA Mechanical Aptitude | 29 | | | | | | | | | | | | | | | |
| 14. Wesman Personnel Classification Test | 24 | | | | | | | | | | | | | | | |
| **E. INTELLIGENCE TESTS** | | | | | | | | | | | | | | | | |
| 1. Analysis of Relationship | 11 | | | | | | | | | | | | | | | |
| 2. Boehm Test of Basic Concepts | 24 | | | | | | | | | | | | | | | |
| 3. California Test of Mental Maturity | 8 | | | | | | | | | | | | | | | |
| 4. Culture Fair IQ Scales I, II, & III Tests of "G" | 20 | | | | | | | | | | | | | | | |
| 5. Full Range Picture Vocabulary Test | 26 | | | | | | | | | | | | | | | |
| 6. Henmon-Nelson Test of Mental Ability | 19 | | | | | | | | | | | | | | | |
| 7. Kuhlman-Anderson Test | 23 | | | | | | | | | | | | | | | |
| 8. Otis Quick Scoring Mental Ability Test | 18 | | | | | | | | | | | | | | | |
| 9. Otis-Lennon Mental Ability Test | 18 | | | | | | | | | | | | | | | |
| 10. Slosson Intelligence Test | 31 | | | | | | | | | | | | | | | |
| 11. SRA Pictorial Reasoning | 29 | | | | | | | | | | | | | | | |
| 12. SRA Short Test of Educational Ability | 29 | | | | | | | | | | | | | | | |
| 13. SRA Test of General Ability | 29 | | | | | | | | | | | | | | | |
| 14. SRA Verbal and Non-Verbal | 29 | | | | | | | | | | | | | | | |
| 15. The D-48 Test | 11 | | | | | | | | | | | | | | | |
| 16. Thurstone Test of Mental Alertness | 29 | | | | | | | | | | | | | | | |

GRADE LEVEL

## TEST FILING SYSTEM

| TEST | CODE NO. |
|---|---|
| **F. INTEREST INVENTORIES** | |
| 1. California Occupational Preference System | 29 |
| 2. California Occupational Preference System Inventory | 13 |
| 3. Career Maturity Inventory | 8 |
| 4. Educational Interest Inventory | 14 |
| 5. Gordon Occupational Check List | 18 |
| 6. Hall Occupational Orientation Inventory | 30 |
| 7. Kuder General Interest Survey | 29 |
| 8. Kuder Vocational Preference | 29 |
| 9. Minnesota Vocational Interest | 24 |
| 10. Occupational Interest Inventory | 29 |
| 11. Ohio Vocational Interest Survey | 24 |
| 12. Picture Interest Inventory | 8 |
| 13. Planning Career Goals | 8 |
| 14. Self-Directed Search (Holland) | 11 |
| 15. Social and Prevocational Information Battery | 8 |
| 16. Vocational Apperception Test | 26 |
| 17. Vocational Preference Inventory | 11 |
| 18. What Could I Be | 29 |
| 19. What I Like to Do | 29 |
| 20. Wide Range Interest-Opinion Test | 17 |
| 21. Work Environment Schedule | 24 |
| 22. Work Values Inventory | 19 |
| **G. PERSONALITY** | |
| 1. California Test of Personality | 8 |
| 2. California Psychological Inventory | 11 |
| 3. Children's Personality Questionnaire | 20 |
| 4. Clinical Analysis Questionnaire | 20 |
| 5. Depression Adjective Check Lists | 13 |
| 6. Early School Personality Inventory | 20 |
| 7. Edwards Personal Preference Schedule | 24 |
| 8. Edwards Personality Inventory | 29 |

*Grade level columns (across the chart): K, 1, 2, 3, 4, 5, 6, 7, 8, 9, 10, 11, 12, College, Adult.*

TEST FILING SYSTEM

| TEST | CODE NO. |
|---|---|
| **G. PERSONALITY** (cont.) | |
| 9. Eysenck Personality Inventory | 13 |
| 10. Fear Survey Schedule | 13 |
| 11. FIRO -- F | 11 |
| 12. Gordon Personal Profile and Personal Inventory | 24 |
| 13. High School Personality Test | 20 |
| 14. How Well Do You Know Yourself? | 27 |
| 15. IPAT Anxiety Scale Questionnaire | 20 |
| 16. Jesness Inventory | 11 |
| 17. Junior Eysenck Personality Inventory | 13 |
| 18. K-D Proneness Check List (Revised) | 34 |
| 19. Kuder Personal | 29 |
| 20. Martin Suicide and Depression Inventory | 27 |
| 21. Minnesota Counseling Inventory | 24 |
| 22. Mooney Problem Check List | 24 |
| 23. Motivation Analysis Test | 20 |
| 24. Multiple Affect Adjective Check List | 13 |
| 25. Neuroticism Scale Questionnaire (NSQ) | 20 |
| 26. Omnibus Personality Inventory | 24 |
| 27. Orientation Inventory | 11 |
| 28. Personal Orientation Inventory | 13 |
| 29. Personnel Reaction Blank | 11 |
| 30. Personality Research Form | 28 |
| 31. Piers-Harris Children's Self Concept Scale | 10 |
| 32. Profile of Mood States | 13 |
| 33. Rotter Incomplete Sentences Blank | 24 |
| 34. Sixteen Personality Factor Questionnaire (16PF) | 20 |
| 35. SRA Personal Audit | 29 |
| 36. SRA Survey of Interpersonal Values | 29 |
| 37. SRA Survey of Personal Value | 29 |
| 38. State-Trait Anxiety Inventory | 11 |
| 39. State-Trait Anxiety Inventory Children (Spielberger) | 11 |

GRADE LEVEL columns: K, 1, 2, 3, 4, 5, 6, 7, 8, 9, 10, 11, 12, College, Adult (ranges indicated by bars in the grid)

# TEST FILING SYSTEM

| TEST | CODE NO. | K | 1 | 2 | 3 | 4 | 5 | 6 | 7 | 8 | 9 | 10 | 11 | 12 | College | Adult |
|------|----------|---|---|---|---|---|---|---|---|---|---|----|----|----|---------|-------|
| **G. PERSONALITY (cont.)** | | | | | | | | | | | | | | | | |
| 40.  Study of Values (Allport) | 19 | | | | | | | | | | | | — | — | — | — |
| 41.  Taylor-Johnson Temperament Analysis | 25 | | | | | | | | — | — | — | — | — | — | — | — |
| 42.  Tennessee Self Concept Scale | 10 | | | | | | | — | — | — | — | — | — | — | — | — |
| 43.  Thorndike Dimensions of Temperament | 24 | | | | | | | | | | | | — | — | — | |
| 44.  Thurston Temperament Schedule | 29 | | | | | | | | | — | — | — | — | — | — | — |
| **H. MISCELLANEOUS TESTS** | | | | | | | | | | | | | | | | |
| 1.  A Psychoeducational Inventory of Basic Learning Abilities | 11 | — | — | — | — | | | | | | | | | | | |
| 2.  Animal Cracker: A Test of Motivation to Achieve | 8 | — | | | | | | | | | | | | | | |
| 3.  Auditory Discrimination Test | 21 | — | — | | | | | | | | | | | | | |
| 4.  First Grade Screening Test | 2 | | — | | | | | | | | | | | | | |
| 5.  Frostig Movement Skills Test Battery | 11 | | | | | — | — | — | | | | | | | | |
| 6.  Survey of Study Habits and Attitudes | 24 | | | | | | | | — | — | — | — | — | — | | |
| 7.  Time Appreciation Test | 34 | | | | | | | — | — | — | — | — | — | — | — | — |
| 8.  Torrance Tests of Creative Thinking | 23 | — | — | — | — | — | — | — | — | — | — | — | — | — | — | — |
| 9.  Watson-Glaser Critical Thinking Appraisal | 24 | | | | | | | | | | — | — | — | — | — | — |
| 10.  Wesman Personal Classification Test | 24 | | | | | | | | | | | | | | — | — |
| 11.  Wide Range Intelligence and Personality Test | 17 | | | | — | — | — | — | — | — | — | — | — | — | | |
| **I. READING TESTS** | | | | | | | | | | | | | | | | |
| 1.  Diagnostic Reading Test | 9 | | — | — | — | — | — | — | — | — | — | — | — | — | | |
| 2.  Diagnostic Reading Scales-Spache | 8 | | — | — | — | — | — | — | — - | - - | - - | - - | - - | - - | | |
| 3.  Durrell-Sullivan Reading Capacity Achievement Test | 18 | | — | — | — | — | — | | | | | | | | | |
| 4.  Durrell Analysis of Reading Difficulty | 18 | | — | — | — | — | — | — | | | | | | | | |
| 5.  Gates-MacGinitie Reading Tests | 19 | | — | — | — | — | — | — | — | — | — | — | — | | | |
| 6.  Iowa Silent Reading Test | 24 | | — | — | — | — | — | — | — | — | — | — | — | | | |
| 7.  Lee-Clark Reading Test | 8 | | — | — | | | | | | | | | | — | | |
| 8.  Metropolitan Readiness Test | 24 | — | — | | | | | | | | | | | | | |

TEST FILING SYSTEM

| TEST | CODE NO. | K | 1 | 2 | 3 | 4 | 5 | 6 | 7 | 8 | 9 | 10 | 11 | 12 | College | Adult |
|---|---|---|---|---|---|---|---|---|---|---|---|---|---|---|---|---|
| | | | | | | | | | GRADE LEVEL | | | | | | | |
| **I. READING TESTS (cont.)** | | | | | | | | | | | | | | | | |
| 9. Murphy-Durrell Reading Readiness Analysis | 24 | | | | | | | | | | | | | | | |
| 10. Nelson-Denny Reading Test | 19 | | | | | | | | | | | | | | | |
| 11. SRA Reading Record | 29 | | | | | | | | | | | | | | | |
| 12. Stanford Diagnostic Reading Test | 24 | | | | | | | | | | | | | | | |
| **J. MARITAL ADJUSTMENT** | | | | | | | | | | | | | | | | |
| 1. A Dating Problems Checklist | 16 | | | | | | | | | | | | | | | |
| 2. El Senoussi Mult. Marital Inventory | 34 | | | | | | | | | | | | | | | |
| 3. Marital Roles Inventory | 34 | | | | | | | | | | | | | | | |
| 4. Marriage Adjustment Inventory | 34 | | | | | | | | | | | | | | | |
| 5. Pair Attraction Inventory | 13 | | | | | | | | | | | | | | | |
| 6. Sex Knowledge Inventory | 16 | | | | | | | | | | | | | | | |

## LIST OF TEST PUBLISHERS

1. The American Council on Education
   I Dupont Circle
   Washington, D.C.  20036

2. American Guidance Service, Inc.
   Publishers' Building
   Circle Pines, Minn.  55014

3. Armed Forces Vocational Testing Group
   Randolph AFB, TX  78148

4. Association Press
   291 Broadway
   New York, NY  10007

5. The Bobbs-Merrill Co., Inc.
   4300 West 62nd St.
   Indianapolis, Ind.  46268

6. Bureau of Educational Measurements
   Emporia Kansas State College
   Emporia, Kansas  66801

7. Bureau of Educational Research and Service
   University of Iowa
   Iowa City, Iowa  52242

8. California Test Bureau
   Del Monte Research Park
   Monterey, CA  93940

9. Committee on Diagnostic Reading Tests, Inc.
   Mountain Home, NC  28758

10. Counselor Recordings and Tests
    Box 6184 Acklen Station
    Nashville, TN  37242

11. Consulting Psychologists Press, Inc.
    577 College Avenue
    Palo Alto, CA  94306

12. Cooperative Test Division
    Educational Testing Service
    Princeton, NJ  08540

13. Edits/Educational and Industrial Testing Service
    P.O. Box 7234
    San Diego, CA  92107

14. Educational Guidance, Inc.
    P.O. Box 511
    Main Post Office
    Dearborn, MI  48121

15. Educational Testing Service
    Addison-Wesley Publishing Co., Inc.
    2725 Sand Hill Road
    Menlo Park, CA  94025

16. Family Life Publications, Inc.
    P.O. Box 427
    Saluda, NC  28773

17. Guidance Associates of Delaware, Inc.
    1526 Gilpin Ave.
    Wilmington, Delaware  19806

18. Harcourt Brace Jovanovich, Inc.
    757 Third Ave.
    New York, NY  10017

19. Houghton Mifflin Co.
    1 Beacon St.
    Boston, MA  02107

20. Institute for Personality and Ability Testing
    P.O. Box 188
    Champaign, IL  61820

21. Language Research Associates, Inc.
    P.O. Box 2085
    Palm Springs, CA  92262

22. National Institute for Personnel Research
    P.O. Box 10319
    Johannesburg, Republic of South Africa

23. Personnel Press, Education Center
    P.O. Box 2649
    Columbus, OH  43216

24. The Psychological Corporation
    757 Third Ave.
    New York, NY  10017

25. Psychological Publications, Inc.
    5300 Hollywood Blvd.
    Los Angeles, CA  90027

26. Psychological Test Specialists
    Box 9229
    Missoula, Montana  59801

27.    Psychologists and Educators, Inc.
       Suite 212
       211 West State St.
       Jacksonville, IL  62650

28.    Research Psychologists Press, Inc.
       P.O. Box 984
       Port Huron, MI  48060

29.    Science Research Associates, Inc.
       155 North Wacker Drive
       Chicago, IL  60606

30.    Scholastic Testing Service, Inc.
       480 Meyer Road
       Bensenville, IL  60106

31.    Slosson Educational Publications, Inc.
       140 Pine St.
       East Aurora, NY  14052

32.    Stanford University Press
       Stanford, CA  94305

33.    Teacher's College Press
       1234 Amsterdam Ave.
       New York, NY  10027

34.    Western Psychological Services
       12031 Wilshire Blvd.
       Los Angeles, CA  90025

*Sources of Further Information:*

American Psychological Association. (1974). *Standards for educational and psychological tests*. Washington, DC: Author.

Buros, O. K. (Ed.) (1978). *The eighth mental measurements yearbook*. Lincoln: University of Nebraska, Buros Institute of Mental Measurement. (The previous seven editions of this Yearbook may be helpful to you.)

Glaser, R., & Bond, L. (Eds.). (1981). Testing: Concepts, policy, practice and research (Special issue). *American Psychologist, 36*(10).

Lyman, H. B. (1963). *Test scores and what they mean*. Englewood Cliffs, NJ: Prentice-Hall.

# SECTION VI

## WRITING TEST REPORTS

MASTERING effective test reporting is one of the primary responsibilities of a counselor. Perhaps the essence of this responsibility lies in the way in which the counselor communicates test results. This section was designed to help counselors write reports based on test results. In this respect, it illustrates how a test report can be organized and how test results can be reported.

# WRITING A TEST REPORT

| | | Tests Administered |
|---|---|---|
| **Name:** | Jan Smith* | 1. SRA Verbal Test |
| **Age:** | 17 | 2. SRA Non-Verbal Test |
| **Status:** | High School Senior | 3. Raven Progressive Matrices |
| **Presenting Problem:** | Selection of College | 4. Kuder Preference Record-Vocational (Form CH) |
| **Priority:** | Career Counseling | 5. Kuder Preference Record-Personal (Form AH) |
| | | 6. How Well Do You Know Yourself |
| | | 7. NSQ Questionnaire |
| | | 8. 16 Personality Factor Test (Form A) |

## Background Information

Jan was referred for counseling services by her parents. At the time of referral she was enrolled as a senior at Central High School in Washington, Mississippi.

Jan has had some practical experience as a part-time typist in one of the local banks and has decided on a career in business. Those courses which she most enjoys are in business; those which she least enjoys are in mathematics and science. She has one brother 14 years of age and one sister 7 years of age.

Tests were selected on the basis of her personal interest in business and her desire to review specific majors within the area of business. A second reason for testing was to develop a broader perspective regarding the selection of a university which could supply the most appropriate training courses for the amount of money she had as an allowance.

## Personal Observations

Jan is well groomed, extremely polite and has appreciated a real popularity among the children with whom she baby-sits. As a baby-sitter, she is extremely innovative. She carries her own games and toys with her in what she refers to as Jan's "happy bag." The youngsters with whom she sits can select from the bag those things with which they want to play.

As a student, Jan has had individual intelligence tests on two occasions. Both scores are quite high. By contrast, her achievement record is average.

*The name has been changed to protect the client.

Because her parents are university graduates and she herself is intelligent and fluent, we have hypothesized that the incongruency between her potential for academic achievement and her actual academic achievement (GPA = C) is something which should be explored.

### Intelligence

Jan took three ability tests under our supervision:

(a) **The SRA Verbal Test**. The SRA Verbal Test was developed after many years of research. It is a test of general intelligence and measures the overall general ability and flexibility of an individual in adjusting to the many complex situations that arise in everyday living. The test is designed to take into account the quickness and accuracy with which a person responds and the potential of the person to prepare in advance for difficulties that might arise to hinder the accomplishment of an assigned task.

(b) **The SRA Non-Verbal Test**. This test uses items supported by research to measure a person's ability to reason out differences in pictured (non-verbal) objects. Research supports the hypothesis that the recognition of differences is basic to learning.

(c) **The Raven Progressive Matrices**. This instrument reflects on a person's capacity to apprehend meaningless figures presented for observation, see the relation between them, and by so doing, develop a systematic method of reasoning. The scale consists of 60 problems divided into five sets of twelve. In each set the first problem is as nearly as possible, self-evident. The problems which follow become progressively more difficult. The five sets provide five opportunities for grasping the method and five progressive assessments of a person's capacity for intellectual activity. A person's total score provides an index of his/her intellectual capacity, whatever his/her nationality or education.

In the case of Jan, the scores from these three instruments are fairly consistent. Jan functions at a high level of intelligence. Further, she seems to find performance type items a little easier than verbal type items. Then too, some intra-test variability was noted on each of the three instruments, i.e. Jan missed several relatively easy questions and successfully completed more difficult ones. This could indicate a tendency to be impulsive. If Jan is impulsive, it could affect her success as a student and ultimately her success as a businesswoman. To cross validate this hypothesis, it is necessary to check Component F on the NSQ and Factor F on the Sixteen Factor Personality Questionnaire (16PF). It appears at this point that she may be functioning at an achievement level below her potential because she is impulsive, i.e. she creates situations (asks questions) which appear offensive and/or responds to test items without thinking carefully about the consequences. One might ask, "Wouldn't she do poorly on the intelligence test if she responded impulsively?" The answer, of course, is "yes!" It is our contention that her score on the intelligence test could be higher than it is.

Our strategy will be to examine Jan's background, interests, and personality characteristics in an effort to determine how we could help her to pursue her academic objectives with a minimal amount of distraction. Ethically we are bound to help her to establish the best possible understanding of her potential and any distractors which could abort her efforts (see Section IV — Principle #6 — Welfare of the Consumer).

### Interest Inventory

(a) **The Kuder Preference Record-Vocational**. This is an instrument designed to discover a person's major interest areas. A score which falls above the 75th percentile is interpreted as identifying an area of significant interest. A score which falls below the 25th percentile is considered an area in which the person lacks interest. Scores ranging from the 26th to the 74th percentile are considered areas of normal or average interest. The client's interests in rank order are:

| | |
|---|---|
| Persuasive | 90th percentile |
| Mechanical | 77th percentile |
| Social Service | 76th percentile |
| Clerical | 72nd percentile |
| Artistic | 62nd percentile |
| Musical | 31st percentile |
| Scientific | 26th percentile |
| Literary | 12th percentile |
| Computational | 12th percentile |
| Outdoors | 8th percentile |

(b) **The Kuder Preference Record-Personal**. This inventory tends to show the kind of relations preferred with other people and the situations in which the client prefers to work.

The client's interests in rank order are:

| | |
|---|---|
| Directing others | 69th percentile |
| Working with ideas | 63rd percentile |
| Avoiding conflict | 45th percentile |
| Being active in groups | 40th percentile |
| Familiar and stable situations | 8th percentile |

### Test Results

(a) **How Well Do You Know Yourself?**\* This inventory was designed to faciliate the study and assessment of the individual's self-impressions. The seven-

---

\*Permission to print this material has been granted by The Psychologists & Educators, Incorporated, Jacksonville, Il, c 1974. Please note: We have modified the descriptions of some of the primary factors for the convenience of the reader. For exact descriptions see Jenkins, T. N., Coleman, J. H. and Fagin, H. (1974) Manual of Instructions, pp. 6, 7, & 8.

teen scores represent primary factors. The description or meaning of each scale score is given below. It is in terms of these descriptions rather than in terms of dictionary definitions that the scores for each scale are to be interpreted. The 50th percentile is considered about average.

**Irritability:** A tendency to become annoyed or upset when one feels frustrated by people or conditions.

*Score: 97th percentile.*

**Practicality:** A tendency to think about and to cope with the environment in relation to practical needs.

*Score: 90th percentile.*

**Punctuality:** A tendency toward promptness in meeting schedules and commitments.

*Score: 35th percentile.*

**Novelty-Loving:** A tendency to like the new, such as new decisions or activities.

*Score: 70th percentile.*

**Vocational Assurance:** A tendency to feel confident about earning a living.

*Score: 89th percentile.*

**Cooperativeness:** A tendency to identify oneself with and work with others to achieve common goals.

*Score: 81th percentile.*

**Ambitiousness:** A tendency to strive for personal advancement in the sense of seeking marks of prestige, such as fame, honor, money and influence.

*Score: 83th percentile.*

**Hypercriticalness:** A tendency toward noticing or pointing out the faults, mistakes or shortcomings of others as well as a tendency to overemphasize these faults.

*Score: 8th percentile.*

**Dejection:** A tendency to feel downcast, sad or depressed.

*Score: 28th percentile.*

**General Moral:** A tendency to feel optimistic.

*Score: 25th percentile.*

**Persistence:** A tendency to continue against opposing forces, either outside or within oneself.

*Score: 84th percentile.*

**Nervousness:** A tendency to feel jumpy or tense, sometimes manifested by fidgeting and exhibiting nervous habits.

*Score: 62nd percentile.*

**Seriousness:** A tendency to exhibit an attitude of earnestness and personal responsibility toward one's work or environment.

*Score: 95th percentile.*

**Submissiveness:** A tendency to comply with what others expect one to do and to submit to domination rather than resist it.

*Score: 88th percentile.*

**Impulsiveness:** A tendency to act without careful consideration or deliberation of the consequences.

*Score: 99th percentile.*

**Dynamism:** A tendency to feel lively, energetic or active with a sense of vigor and well-being.

*Score: 59th percentile.*

**Emotional Control:** A tendency to inhibit or restrain socially disapproved emotional reactions such as controlling one's temper or remaining calm when others become upset.

*Score: 17th percentile.*

(b) **The Neuroticism Scale Qestionnaire.**\* The NSQ is an inventory designed to compare deep feelings experienced by normal individuals. The scores given are in stens. The term sten means that the norm population or the scores of all the people to whom the test was administered during its construction were divided into ten (10) standard groups. Scores falling in the 5th and 6th stens are considered falling in the average group.

Jan's scores were as follows:

| | |
|---|---|
| Component I | 9th Sten |
| Component F | 3rd Sten |
| Component E | 6th Sten |
| Anxiousness | 5th Sten |
| Total Composite | 6th Sten |

**Component I.** People with high scores on Component I are tender-minded, sensitive, and fastidious in the sense that women typically have those characteristics when contrasted with men. In fact, the dimension has been called feminity-masculinity, and indeed, some men score significantly higher on this factor than do the general population of men.

An individual's position on this dimension seems to be largely a product of his/her earlier environment, i.e. it has little genetic determination. The present hypothesis regarding Component I is that it represents overprotection and sheltering from the realities of life, often by an unrealistic, in-

---

\*Copyright 1961 by the Institute for Personality and Ability Testing, Inc. Modified and reproduced by permission of the copyright owner.

dulgent home education. The I (+) person tends to be sentimental, kindly, sometimes artistically and otherwise "cultured," and imaginative even to the point of being fanciful. By contrast, low I (–) scoring people might be described as unfeeling "philistines." They are often brusque in manner, tend to lack artistic interest, seem to lack sensitivity at times, and are inclined to be extremely practical. They are no-nonsense types: tough, hard, and responsible.

*Score: 9th Sten.*

**Component F.** People with high scores on Component F show an almost classical picture of depression. Glum, sober, serious, they are taciturn, incommunicative, smug, seclusive, retiring and introspective. Their quietness does not mean serenity, for when (as often) they are upset, they simply simmer and brood, without easily detectable outward signs, such as restlessness.

By contrast, low-scoring people are cheerful, happy-go-lucky, "the life of the party." Such people are humorous, witty, cheerful, enthusiastic, and like excitement and social contact. Sociometric measurements show that they are, in fact, more popular than persons at the depressive pole. Low-scoring people are expressive, sociable, talkative (perhaps too much so), energetic, fast-moving and impulsive. Often, however, their cleverness is only superficial (impressive more for its quickness than its depth) and they are too impulsive in the sense that what they have done hastily needs to be done over again more carefully, or perhaps should never have been done at all. (This suggests one reason why low scoring on this component is generally associated with poorer performance scholastically from grade school through college.)

*Score: 3rd Sten.*

**Component E.** People with high scores on Component E are submissive, obedient, complacent, and dependent. They frequently lack competitive drive and, at times, fail to assert themselves.

People with low scores on this component are dominant, assertive, ascendant, aggressive, and competitive, even pugnacious. The picture is generally quite close to what is usually meant by the term "authoritarian personality."

*Score: 6th Sten.*

**Anxiousness.** The Anxiousness score is a composite of such related factors as guilt proneness, frustration, tension, and emotional immaturity. People who score high on this component have feelings of anxiety, dread, guilt, inferiority, frustration and loneliness. They are easily upset, tense, excitable, restless, irritable, emotionally immature and unstable, with low levels of tolerance for frustration.

Low scoring people show an absence of feelings of anxiety. They are emotionally mature, secure, calm and composed, self-confident, realistic, stable, resilient, and in a broad sense, psychologically healthy.

*Score: 5th Sten.*

**Total Composite.** The total NSQ score is a simple unweighted sum of the raw scores on the four components. Thus, all information in this score is already available in the four components which contribute to it.

*Score: 6th Sten.*

(c) **The Sixteen Personality Factor Questionnaire (16PF).\*** This test was designed to give the broadest coverage of personality possible in the briefest time available.

The scores are distributed over ten equal-interval standard score points from 1 through 10, with the population average at sten 5.5. Stens 5 and 6 extend, respectively, a half standard deviation below and above the average. One would consider stens of 5 or 6 as average, 4 or 7 slightly deviant (respectively in a low and high direction), 2, 3, 8, ad 9 strongly deviant, and 1 or 10 extreme. All sten scores are based on the specific populations used to standardize the 16PF.

The client's scores are as follows:

**Factor A: Reserved vs. Outgoing.** People who score low (sten of 1 to 3) on Factor A tend to be stiff, cool, skeptical and aloof. They like things rather than people, they like working alone, and they attempt to avoid situations in which they have to compromise viewpoints. These people are likely to have rigid standards . . . and to be precise in their ways of doing things. Although this could be a problem in some career areas, there are also some occupations in which these traits are desirable. At times, those who score low also tend to be critical, obstructive or hard.

People who score high (sten of 8 to 10) tend to be good-natured, easygoing, emotionally expressive, ready to cooperate, attentive to people, softhearted and kindly adaptable. They like occupations dealing with people and socially-impressive situations. Such people readily form active groups. They are generous in their personal reactions, less afraid of criticism and better able to remember names of people.

*Score: 8th Sten.*

**Factor B: Concrete-thinking vs. Abstract-thinking.** The person scoring low on Factor B tends to be slow to learn and grasp, dull, and given to concrete and literal interpretations.

The person who scores high on Factor B tends to be quick to grasp ideas and a fast learner.

*Score: 8th Sten.*

---

**Factor C: Affected by Feelings vs. Emotionally Stable.** People who score low on this factor tend to be low in frustration tolerance for unsatisfactory conditions, fretful, easily emotional and annoyed, and active in dissatisfaction.

People who score high on this factor tend to be emotionally mature, stable, realistic about life, unruffled, posses ego strength, and are better able to maintain solid group morale. Sometimes they may be making resigned adjustments to unsolved emotional problems.

*Score: 3rd Sten.*

**Factor E: Humble vs. Assertive.** People who score low on Factor E tend to give way to others, to be docile, and to conform. They are often dependent, confessing, and anxious for obsessional correctness.

People who score high on this factor are assertive, self-assured, and independent minded. They tend to be austere, a law unto themselves, hostile or extrapunitive, authoritarian in manner, and have a disregard for authority.

*Score: 4th Sten.*

**Factor F: Sober vs. Happy-Go-Lucky.** People who score low on Factor F tend to be restrained and introspective. They are sometimes dour, pessimistic, unduly deliberate, and considered smug and primly correct by observers. They tend to be sober, dependable people.

People who score high tend to be cheerful, active, talkative, frank, expressive and carefree. They are frequently chosen as elected leaders. They may be impulsive and mercurial.

*Score: 8th Sten.*

**Factor G: Expedient vs. Conscientious.** People who score low tend to be unsteady in purpose. Such people are often casual and lacking in effort for group undertakings and cultural demands. Their freedom from group influences may, at times, make them more effective but can also lead to antisocial acts. This refusal to be bound by rules causes them to have less somatic upsets from stress.

People who score high on this factor tend to be exacting in character, dominated by a sense of duty, perservering, responsible, planful, and "fill the unforgiven minute." They are usually conscientious and moralistic, and prefer hardworking people to witty companions.

*Score: 4th Sten.*

**Factor H: Shy vs. Venturesome.** People who score low on this triat tend to be shy, withdrawn, cautious, retiring, and "wallflowers." They usually have feelings of inferiority. They also tend to be slow and impeded in speech, dislike occupations with personal contacts, prefer one or two close friends to large groups, and are not given to keeping in contact with all that is going on around them.

People who score high are sociable, bold, ready to try new things, spontaneous and abundant in emotional responses. Such people are "thick-skinned." This toughness enables them to face tremendous wear and tear. However, they can be careless of detail, ignore danger signals and consume much time talking. They tend to be pushy and actively interested in the opposite sex.

*Score: 5th Sten.*

**Factor I: Tough-minded vs. Tender-minded.** People who score low on this factor tend to be practical, realistic, masculine, independent, responsible, but skeptical of subjective cultural elaborations. They are sometimes unmoved, hard, cynical, smug and tend to keep a group operating on a practical and realistic no-nonsense basis.

People who score high on this factor tend to be tender-minded, daydreamers, artistic, and fastidious. Such people are sometimes demanding of attention and help, impatient, dependent, and impractical . . . people who dislike crudeness and rough occupations. They tend to slow up group performance and to upset morale by unrealistic fussiness.

*Score: 8th Sten.*

**Factor L: Trusting vs. Suspicious.** People who score low here tend to be free of jealous tendencies, adaptable, cheerful, uncompetitive, concerned about other people, and good team workers.

People who score high on this factor tend to be mistrustful or doubtful . . . they tend to be ego involved. That is, they tend to be self-opinionated, and interested in internal, mental life. They are poor team members.

*Score: 6th Sten.*

**Factor M: Practical vs. Imaginative.** People who score low on this factor tend to be anxious to do the right things, are attentive to practical matters, and subject to the dictation of what is obviously possible. Such people are concerned over detail, able to keep their heads during emergencies, but sometimes are unimaginative.

People who score high tend to be unconventional, unconcerned over everyday matters, self-motivated, imaginatively-creative, concerned with "essentials" and oblivious to particular people and physical realities. Their inner-directed interests sometimes lead to unrealistic situations accompanied by expressive outbursts. Their individuality tends to cause them personal rejection in group activities.

*Score: 4th Sten.*

**Factor N: Forthright vs. Shrewd.** People who score low tend to be unsophisticated, sentimental, natural and spontaneous. They are sometimes crude and awkward, but are usually content with what comes.

High scoring people on this factor tend to be polished and experienced, worldly, and shrewd. They are often hardheaded and analytical, have an intellectual, unsentimental approach to situations, and are akin to cynicism.

*Score: 6th Sten.*

**Factor O: Placid vs. Apprehensive.** Low-scoring people on this factor tend to be placid, with unshakeable nerve. Such people are unanxiously confident with themselves and their capacity to deal with things. They are resilient and secure almost to the point of being insensitive to others who are not going along with them. This may evoke antipathies and distrust.

High-scoring people on this factor tend to be worriers who are moody, full of foreboding, and brooding. Such people have a tendency to become anxious when in a difficult situation. When in groups, they do not feel accepted by others, nor do they feel free to participate in group settings.

*Score: 7th Sten.*

**Factor $Q_1$: Conservative vs. Experimenting.** People who score low are confident in what they have been taught and accept the "tried and true," despite inconsistencies and/or better alternatives. These people are cautious and compromising in regard to new ideas. They tend to oppose and postpone change, are inclined to go along with tradition, are more conservative in religion and politics and tend not to be interested in analytical "intellectual" thought.

People who score high tend to be interested in "intellectual" matters and have doubts on fundamental issues. Such people are skeptical and inquiring regarding ideas (either old or new). They tend to be more well-informed, less inclined to moralize, more inclined to experiment in life generally, and more tolerant of inconvenience and change.

*Score: 6th Sten.*

**Factor $Q_2$: Group dependent vs. Self-sufficient.** People who score low on this factor prefer to work with and make decisions with other people. They like and depend on social approval and admiration. They tend to go along with the group and may be lacking in individual resolution. They are not necessarily gregarious by choice, but rather, need group support.

People who score high are temperamentally independent, accustomed to going their own way and accustomed to making decisions and taking action on their own. They discount public opinion, but are not necessarily dominant in their relations with others. They do not dislike people, but simply do not need support from others.

*Score: 4th Sten.*

**Factor $Q_3$: Undisciplined Self-conflict vs. Controlled.** People who score low will not be bothered with control and regard for social demands. They are not overly considerate, careful, or painstaking. They may feel maladjusted.

People who score high on this factor tend to have strong control of their emotions and general behavior, are inclined to be socially aware and careful, and evidence what is commonly termed "self-respect" and regard for social reputation. They sometimes tend, however, to be obstinate. Effective leaders are high on this factor.

*Score: 5th Sten.*

**Factor $Q_4$: Relaxed vs. Tense.** People who score low on Factor $Q_4$ tend to be sedate, relaxed, composed and satisfied (not frustrated). In some situations, their oversatisfaction can lead to laziness and low performance in the sense that low motivation produces little trial and error.

Conversely, people who have a level of high tension may find that the tension disrupts their school or work performance. People who score high on this factor tend to be tense, excitable, restless, fretful and impatient. They are often fatigued, but unable to remain inactive. When functioning within groups, they take a poor view of unity, orderliness, and leadership. Their frustration represents an excess of stimulated, but undischarged drive.

*Score: 7th Sten.*

**Creativity.** People who score high on this factor tend to be more creative than those who are of equal ability and academic training, but who are not creative. In other words, the difference between the creative and the routine but competent individual lies far more in the realm of personality differences than in the realm of special ability differences. The creative person is not a simple introvert but is a self-sufficient introvert who might naturally have been an extrovert except for the training received in the typical school and the fact that major inhibiting forces are sometimes utilized to produce "good mixers" and persons with other introversive characteristics. The aim of this scale is to enable psychologists and counselors to adapt test scores to creativity in particular areas. This is done through scholarship selection and guidance work generally designed to pick people who will not merely pass examinations with facility, but will also use these abilities in later life in especially creative ways.

*Score: 6th Sten.*

## *Test Summary*

From the results of her test scores, it appears that Jan is a person of above average intelligence. The point should be stressed that the term, intelligence, is a concept which in its simplest form indicates potential. It does not, however, indicate success will come without effort.

It must also be remembered that ability and interest are not identical and that a person may have ability or potential for an area without possessing any immediate interest in that area. Conversely, it is also true that a person may have an interest in an area while possessing only limited potential for the area.

I. **Vocational Interests.** Jan indicates an interest in work areas that include social service, mechanical, and persuasive triats (Kuder Preference Record-Vocational). Advanced college training is needed for many of the occupational selections listed.

*Social Service-Professional*

Social and Welfare Worker
  Family service workers
  Child welfare workers
  School social workers
  Medical social workers
  Psychiatric social workers
Rehabilitation Counselor
Vocational Counselor

*Persuasive-Professional*

Author; Editor; Reporter
Public Relations Worker
  Department stores
  Hospitals
  Manufacturing firms
  Professional Associations

*Persuasive-Clerical and Kindred*

Adjustment clerk
Information clerk
Agent: appraiser
Insurance saleswoman
Real estate saleswoman
Stock and bond saleswoman
Sales clerk

As an aid in selecting a particular setting in which to function Jan should note that her inventory results (Kuder Preference Record-Personal) indicate a significant interest in situations where she directs others and/or situations in which she has a variety of new experiences.

II. **Personal Exploration.** Since Jan plans to enter college, she may want to explore her personality characteristics and consider the potential impact they may have on her educational plans and vocational decisions. Naturally, it is always in the person's best interests to strive for balance within the realm of personality characteristics, personal interests, and academic abilities. It seems especially important that Jan understand how personality factors support or deter from her stated interests. Relative to this point and within the limitations of our objective information, it might be said that there are five major areas upon which we can focus.

First, Jan is not only above average in intelligence, i.e. she is a person who graps new ideas rapidly and learns quickly. Basically, she learns quickly and likes new challenges.

Second, the client appears to be an extremely sensitive person. Personal observation combined with test results indicate a real interest in people, and considerable concern about how people are treated. The implications here are of course speculative. Another hypothesis might be that Jan is concerned with how others are treated because she is also concerned with how she is treated by others.

Third, although Jan feels confident about her vocational future and her ability to earn a living, she does have some feelings of apprehension about the world at large and her future status in it. However, it should also be noted that there are some indications that this may simply be reflective of her search for identity within the ouside world. Then too, she may be submitting to group demands in an effort to be accepted by others. To react like this is probably somewhat painful to a person who fundamentally desires openness.

Fourth, Jan may, on occasion, find that she has acted out in haste and that in so doing she must do over again more carefully things which should, perhaps, never have been done in the first place. It appears that she acts without careful consideration of the consequences. This could create some rather awkward situations for her. In her academic work she might find herself touching upon her assignments and subject matter areas in a superficial way simple to get the work done. To work in this way becomes incongruent with her academic objectives for it creates situations in which her focus of attention is on expedience rather than quality. That is, because of her desire to become a professional person Jan should consider the advantages of becoming professionally involved in her work. To assume the responsibility for doing a job is an indication of intelligence . . . to accept the responsibility for doing a job, and doing it well, is an indication of maturity. She may find it possible to reverse her attitude of impulsivity by attaching personal values to each job and by so doing see the job in a different perspective. Since what she does is cognitive in origin and since it has much to do with her values, what she must understand is that impulsive moves can, and frequently do, cause greater conflict for the impulsive person than for the recipients of the impulsive acts. It is simply a matter of thinking before plunging.

Fifth, Jan may find that when she is with groups of people her own age she sometimes experiences some feelings of awkwardness. At times she may feel that she is not totally accepted by the group. Impulsively, she may react by attempting to be clever or original. This type of reaction may lead to further awkwardness because Jan's responses may be too open, too free, and perhaps too blunt. To respond openly is not necessarily wrong, but when she does respond she should carefully consider what she is about to say and how it might affect the individuals with whom she is interacting.

III. **Educational Exploration.** Selecting a college to attend is often a difficult task because of the number of factors that must be considered. In reality several colleges could probably serve to provide an education for any given individual, but because each person has a particular set of interests, abilities, and perspectives the "best choice" theory of college selection is important. In other words, there is probably one college, if it can be identified, which is better suited to the needs and values of a given student than are any of the others.

Exploring colleges and universitities was approached in a two step process. First, those factors which Jan determined to be important in selecting a college were formulated. Some of these factors included: (1) location of the college, (2) size of both the college and the local community, (3) requirements for admission, (4) accreditation standing of the college, (5) the presence of a school of business, and (6) whether or not the college was coeducational. Seven out-of-state colleges were found which satisfied all the factors. The seven are listed below. (The client first expressed a desire to attend an out-of-state school.)

> Louisiana State University, Baton Rouge, Louisiana
> University of Southwestern Louisiana, Lafayette, Louisiana
> Memphis State University, Memphis, Tennessee
> University of Tennessee, Knoxville, Tennessee
> North Texas State University, Denton, Texas
> University of Alabama, Tuscaloosa, Alabama
> University of Arkansas, Fayetteville, Arkansas

IV. **Recommendations:** In light of these data the following recommendations are made:

1. That Jan seek the assistance of a counselor to work with her on how to control her impulsive behavior. In this case, it appears that Jan may benefit from a well defined management plan.

2. That Jan obtain a copy of the Occupational Outlook Handbook and other occupational materials in the career development library to obtain specific information about the occupations listed in section I of the *Test Summary*.

3. That Jan obtain copies of the catalogues from the in-state and out-of-state colleges and universitites which appear to be of interest to her. By writing to the Financial Aid Office of each institution Jan can obtain information about financial aid and work study programs.

***Sources of Further Information:***

Hollis, J. W., & Donn, P. A. (1973). *Psychological report writing: Theory and practice.* Muncie, IN: Accelerated Development.

# SECTION VII

## DRUGS

ALTHOUGH it is difficult to estimate the current use of prescribed drugs in the United States, some reports indicate that during any given year over 20,000,000 people use such drugs to cope with depressive disorders, anxiety disorders, and thought disorders. Thus, it seems that it would be in the best interests of counselors to know something about drugs, how they are used, and how to recognize some of the critical residual effects of drug use and abuse.

## Subsection A

## PRESCRIBED DRUGS

NATURALLY, the person best equipped to prescribe drugs for affective disorders is a psychiatrist. As a result, many counselors feel that the best solution to drug treatment is to refer clients with drug problems to a physician or psychiatrist. However, one of the primary difficulties with such a solution is that medical doctors, especially psychiatrists, are not always easily available for referral. When a psychiatrist is available, however, referral or consultation is always the best solution and most ethical course of action. There are, of course, some ways in which the counselor can improve referral procedures and expedite treatment when it is needed. One way of doing this is for the counselor to learn what side effects to look for and what those side effects mean in terms of referral and treatment.

### Major Tranquilizers

For example, counselors should know that major tranquilizers or antipsychotics as they are sometimes called, normalize psychomotor activity and reduce mental agitation, i.e. psychotic thinking and suspiciousness. They are usually prescribed for schizophrenic type disorders, manic disorders, arteriosclerosis and some psychoses experienced by children. Major tranquilizers are also prescribed for patients who are on the verge of delirium tremors, a physical reaction which sometimes appears when excessive use of alcohol is discontinued or considerably reduced. Thus, what the counselor should know is that major tranquilizers potentiate alcohol and that alcohol potentiates the residual effects of tranquilizers. Translated in terms of physiological reactions what that means is that alcohol intensifies the effect of the tranquilizer and that tranquilizers intensify the impact of alcohol. The bottom line, of course, is that drugs and drinking (alcohol) do *not* mix.

Second, the counselor should understand that major tranquilizers do precisely what you might expect them to do; they reduce mental alertness and slow down psychomotor coordination. People who use such drugs should not engage in activities which might be dangerous to themselves or others. That is, patients who are taking major tranquilizers should not drive nor should they be operating dangerous equipment or power tools.

So that counselors might recognize some of the most frequently used major tranquilizers a listing of some of those drugs and their side effects are included. A more comprehensive listing of major tranquilizers and a detailed explanation of the residual effects of these drugs can be found in the references listed at the end of this section.

## Chemical Classes of Antipsychotics (Major Tranquilizers)

| Classification and Generic Name | Brand Name | Usual Oral Daily Dose Range |
|---|---|---|
| A. Phenothiazines: | | |
| 1) Aliphatics | | |
| Chlorpromazine | Thorazine | 200 -1000 mg. |
| Triflupromazine | Vesprin | |
| 2) Piperadines | | |
| Thioridazine | Mellaril | 200 - 800 mg. |
| Mesoridazine | Serentil | 100 - 400 mg. |
| 3) Piperazines | | |
| Trifluoperazine | Stelazine | |
| Fluphenazine | Prolixin, Permitil | 2 -   15 mg. |
| Perphenazine | Trilafon | |
| B. *Thioxanthenes* | | |
| Thiothixene | Navane | 2 -   15mg. |

C. *Butyrophenones*

Haloperidol (Haldol): Is known by the generic name Haloperidol. Dosage is 2-15 mg. per day. The drug is produced by McNeil. The tablets are circular shaped and uncoated. White = ½ mg., yellow = 1 mg., lavender = 2 mg., green = 5 mg. and blue = 10 mg.

| D. *Dibenzoxazepines* | | |
|---|---|---|
| Loxapine | Loxitane | 60 - 100 mg. |
| E. *Dihydroindolones* | | |
| Molindone | Moban | 50 - 225 mg. |

## General Statement

When first taking major tranquilizers, patients frequently feel sleepy, have slurred speech, and lack mental alertness. After several weeks this feeling should subside. If it *does not,* the patient should check with his or her physician.

Other undesirable side effects include experiencing a chill, fainting, rapid heartbeat, and nasal congestion. In some cases neuralgia (nerve pain), and in other cases a decreased sensitivity to pain (a condition which can lead to serious injury) is evident.

Major tranquilizers also cause endocrine disorders such as enlarged breasts, production of milk, amenorreha (a woman's monthly bleeding stops), and menstrual irregularities.

Then, too, there can be a form of dermatitis which is marked by a reddening of the skin (sometimes in patches) and is frequently accompanied by severe itching.

The patient taking major tranquilizers may develop *photosensitivity* (sunburns easily); *agranulocytosis* (fever, sore throat, extreme fatigue, sores, bleeding of the skin and easy bruising); *Akathesia* (motor restlessness); *Dyskinesia* (peculiar tongue, face and eye distortions); *Extrapyramida Crisis* (profuse sweating, difficulty with breathing, skin color turns blue, drooling and change in blood pressure); *Parkinsonism* (psychomotor retardation, rigidity of muscles, shuffling gait, and a mask-like appearance).

## Minor Tranquilizers

The counselor should also know something about minor tranquilizers or antianxiety drugs as they are sometimes called. Minor tranquilizers are used primarily to reduce anxiety. They do this by sedating a person and easing the feelings of insecurity that usually accompany anxiety. Interestingly enough, they can produce a condition of drug dependency and when a patient is suddenly withdrawn from high doses will frequently cause residual effects such as anxiety, convulsions, restlessness and/or weakness. Although, the side effects are usually less dangerous than they are with major tranquilizers, the patient should know that addiction is possible and that patients should not drink, drive, nor operate power tools while using these drugs.

Some of the more frequently used minor tranquilizers are:

| Classification and Generic Name | Brand Name | Usual Oral Daily Dose Range |
|---|---|---|
| A. *Benzodiazepines* | | |
| Chlordiazepoxide | Librium | 15 - 300 mg. |
| Diazepam | Valium | 5 - 60 mg. |
| Lorazipam | Ativan | 1 - 10 mg. |
| Chlorazepate | Tranxene | 15 - 60 mg. |
| Alprazolam | Xanax | 0.5 - 1.5 mg. |
| Prazipam | Centrax | 20 - 60 mg. |
| B. *Glycerol Derivatives* | | |
| Meprobamate | Equanil, Miltown | 800 - 3200mg. |
| C. *Diphenyl Methane Derivative (Antihistamines)* | | |
| Hydroxyzine | Atarax, Vistaril | 75 - 400 mg. |

It should be noted that the therapeutic dose is considerably lower than the amount required for addiction. An estimate on addictive use for something so frequently prescribed as Valium would be 75 mg. per day; lethal dosage would be approximately 700 mg. Although such drugs are used in suicide attempts, many of the attempts fail.

Less effective among the minor tranquilizers are the antihistamines. They are sometimes used because the side effects are less undesirable. However, prolonged use of these drugs at high dosages can produce dependence. Then too, sudden withdrawal can result in such things as: Insomnia, Anorexia, and Gastrointestinal Distress.

## Antidepressants

Antidepressants are drugs which relieve depression. Unlike stimulants which elevate moods, the antidepressant is a drug which improves a state of agitation or anxiety without overstimulating the patient.

Some of the characteristics which typify depression are feelings of hopelessness, remorse, rejection, and despair. Sometimes the person will talk about suicide. At other times, the person may simply withdraw from active participation with others, and may exhibit a loss of appetite, a weight change and/or a problem with insomnia. When any of these symptoms occur, the counselor should suspect depression. If the person is on antidepressive drugs but continues to exhibit such characteristics, the chances are that the person may be experiencing situational or reactive depression (i.e., is experiencing depression over a recent loss or death in the family) or needs a dosage adjustment.

There are two major areas of classification for antidepressant drugs: Tricyclics, and MAO Inhibitors.

Tricyclics are recognized as safer and are perhaps more useful because MAO inhibitors when combined with certain types of food such as sour cream, yogurt, chicken liver, soy sauce, canned figs, chocolate, aged cheese, raisins, pickled herring, beer or wine, can result in death.

### *Classification and Usual Daily Dosage Range for the Drugs Used in the Treatment of Affective Disorders*

DEPRESSION

| Classification and Generic Name | Brand Name | Usual Oral Daily Dose Range | |
|---|---|---|---|
| | | Acute | Maintenance |
| A. *Tricyclic Antidepressants* | | | |
| 1. *Tertiary Amines* | | | |
| Amitriptyline | Elavil, Endep | 150-300 mg. | 50-150 mg. |
| Doxepin | Sinequan | 150-300 mg. | 50-150 mg. |
| Imipramine | Tofranil | 150-300 mg. | 50-150 mg. |
| 2. *Secondary Amines* | | | |
| Nortriptyline | Aventyl, Pamelor | 100-150 mg. | 50- 75 mg. |
| Desipramine | Norpramin | 100-250 mg. | 50-100 mg. |
| Protriptyline | Vivactil | 10- 60 mg. | 10- 30 mg. |

B. *Monoamine Oxidase Inhibitors*
   1. *Hydrazine*

| | | | |
|---|---|---|---|
| Phenelzine | Nardil | 15 - 60 mg. | 10 - 30 mg. |

   2. *Non-hydrazine*

| | | | |
|---|---|---|---|
| Tranylcypromine | Parnate | 10 - 60 mg. | 10 - 30 mg. |

C. *Stimulants*

| | | | |
|---|---|---|---|
| Amphetamine | Benzedrine, Dexedrine, | 10 - 30 mg. | 5 - 15 mg. |
| Methylphenidate | Ritalin | 20 - 60 mg. | 10 - 30 mg. |

The minimum effective dosage of Tricyclics for those under 65 years of age is usually about 100 mg. per day. Both MAO inhibitors and Tricyclics intensify the effects of alcohol, reduce mental alertness and slow down psychomotor coordination. Counselors should note that Tricyclics produce side effects that are sometimes troublesome. This includes but is not limited to such things as constipation, difficulty in urinating, dizziness, dry mouth and stuffy nose. Other undesirable side effects of antidepressants consist of such things as high fever, voracious appetite, blurred vision, rapid heart beat, increased anger, mental confusion, depersonalization, headache, heartburn, stomach pains, abnormal sex drive, pale skin, pink skin, yellow skin, nonhealing sores and easy bruising.

When such symptoms occur and the person is on antidepressants, it may be the drug which is creating the symptoms. Referral to a medical doctor for corrections is imperative.

## Present Psychiatric Treatment Models

### Psychoanalytic and Cognitive Models

Although some psychiatrists still use and support the psychoanalytic or cognitive models of therapy (i.e., the idea that primary disturbances in thinking are caused by repression or lead to the development of a disturbed mood state) the general trend is to use chemotherapy.

The most current treatment models in psychiatry appear to be the *Biogenic Amine Model, Endocrine Model, Electrolyte Model,* and *Genetic Model.* In brief, these are as follows:

### Biogenic Amine Model

The Biogenic Amine Model deals primarily with neurotransmission and some of the physiological effects which result when abnormal transmission occurs. At the center of this theory is the belief that catecholamines (epinephrine, norepinephrine and dopamine) and indole amines (serotonin and histamine) play a significant role in the genesis of depression. The idea is that a decrease in the level of amines in the brain causes depression. To correct this condition the psychiatrist recommends two classes of drugs which will increase the level of amines, MAO inhibitors (Monoamine oxadase inhibitor) and Tricyclics.

### Endocrine Model

The Endocrine Model is based on the idea that the neuroendocrine cells which secrete hypothalamic-releasing hormones are regulated by monoamenergic neural tracts. It is further hypothesized that there is increased adrenocortical activity in those who are depressed or anxious and that this activity is caused by the malfunctioning of the hypothalamus and its ability to control the pituitary function. As a result, an excessive amount of ACTH (adrenocorticotropic hormone) is released into the system. Essentially what happens is that brain catecholamines regulate the release of pituitary hormones. Noradrenergic neurons stimulate release of the corticotropin-releasing factor (CRF) which in turn is transported by a venous shunt to the pituitary. This stimulates a release of ACTH. If the release is excessive, it leads to hypersecretion of adrenal corticoids. Excessive cortisol may, in turn, cause a deficit in norepinephrine which leads to depression.

### Electrolyte Model

The electrolyte model is based on the idea that several important electrolytes (sodium and potassium) seem to experience a redistribution. Although potassium does not change significantly, it is hypothesized that increased intracellular sodium may be present in patients with psychotic depression and that after clinical recovery there is a corresponding decrease in sodium. It is further suggested that these changes result from a redistribution of the electrolytes within the body and not from a change in the total body concentration of sodium and potassium.

### Genetic Model

The Genetic Model is based on the idea that there is a genetic basis for the development of depression and that depression results from a genetic predisposition to the disorder.

## Summary

In summary one might say that psychiatrists are moving toward a chemically based therapy in which the amine hypothesis is central to many of the models which describe biochemical changes. The theory is predicated on the idea that within the brain, a delicate biochemical equilibrium exists. External environmental contingencies and/or internal peripheral dysfunctions sometimes upset this balance. Central to this hypothesis is the belief that any stressor of a chronic nature results in an increase of ACTH and plasma cortisol. This inhibits neural functioning through raising threshold potential. Concomitantly, a deficiency of noradrenalin and serotonin is developed within the neuron which ultimately results in depression.

## Subsection B

## DRUG ABUSE

AMONG those drugs most frequently abused today are barbituates, amphetamines, marijuana, narcotic-analgesics (such as heroin and morphine), and hallucinogenics (such as LSD, Mescaline and Phencyclidine — PCP). Abuse is the use of a drug for reasons other than that for which it is normally prescribed. The purpose in misusing it is to gain residual effects which have nothing to do with medical treatment.

**Barbituates:** For example, barbituates interfere with cells in the brain which are responsible for alertness. When misused, barbituates are taken to produce a kind of intoxication (the person uses them to get "stoned"). People who use drugs in this way attempt to anesthesize themselves against the outside world by decreasing their alertness to outside stimuli. Should you (as a counselor) find a person who appears to be addicted, *DO NOT encourage the addicted person to go "Cold Turkey"*. This can result in his or her death. The person needs medical attention and should be placed in a hospital where he or she can be withdrawn gradually and safely.

**Amphetamines:** Amphetamines, unlike barbituates, are central nervous system stimulants. They increase heart rate, cause sweating and loss of appetite, dilate pupils, produce euphoria, cause paranoid feelings and create nervousness and irritability. Although they are sometimes prescribed for weight reduction, their use as appetite suppressors is shortlived and extended use has been found to cause depression and possible psychosis. Withdrawal is difficult because it produces both auditory and visual hallucinations, paranoid psychosis, depression and extreme fatigue. Due to the serious side effects caused by withdrawal (depression and psychosis), the addicted person should be referred to a drug and/or medical treatment setting in which he or she can be carefully monitored. Referral will not remove those feelings of depression which normally accompany withdrawal but will help the person through a period during which suicide becomes a high risk factor.

**Cocaine:** The effects of cocaine are very much like those of amphetamines. Unlike amphetamines, cocaine does not create a physical dependency. However, the psychological dependence it creates is overwhelming and anyone found using it should be referred for appropriate medical treatment.

**Narcotic-Analgesics:** Narcotic-analgesics are powerful pain relievers. They include such drugs as morphine, heroin, codeine, darvon, demerol and percodan. People misuse them to gain a feeling of euphoria. Some of these drugs, such as heroin and morphine, produce a marked constriction of the pupils. Demerol, however, produces a dilation of the pupils. Users sometimes wear sunglasses both inside and outside to avoid detection. They also wear long sleeves to hide needle tracks.

The person withdrawing from use experiences such things as tearing, yawning and nose dripping symptoms during the first twelve hours. During the second twelve hours the person experiences chills, hot and cold flashes, muscle cramps, and muscle twitches. During the third and fourth twelve-hour periods, the person experiences vomiting, diarrhea, excessive back and leg pains and loss of appetite. After three days, many of these symptoms will subside.

Although a person addicted to narcotic-analgesics can go "cold turkey" it is best to refer the person to a drug detoxification center for help.

**Hallucinogenics:** Hallucinogenics alter a person's moods and perceptions. They are usually taken orally and almost always produce euphoria accompanied by visual illusions. People who use such drugs are sometimes plagued by "flashbacks," i.e. illusions, delusions and/or hallucinations, which accompanied the original onset.

Those who are found using such drugs should be referred for appropriate medical care. Long term residual effects include protracted psychotic disturbances which resemble schizophrenia.

## Subsection C

## ALCOHOLISM

Alcohol is a depressant. As such it slows down the functions of the central nervous system and creates the same general effect on the body as barbituates, analgesics, antihistamines and opiates. When consumed with major tranquilizers, minor tranquilizers or antidepressants, it intensifies the effect of these drugs and at worst, can create death by respiratory arrest.

To determine whether or not a client is taking the first steps toward addiction, the counselor should look for the following symptoms:

(a) When consuming alcohol, does the client gulp his or her drinks?
(b) Does the client exercise a preference for companions who drink?
(c) Does the client begin drinking in the morning?
(d) Does the client drink surreptitiously?
(e) Does the client exercise repeated absenteeism from work or school?
(f) Does the client drink to reduce tension, anger, social discomfort or depression?
(g) Is the client involved in frequent automobile accidents?

Once the client is alcholic, the following symptoms become more obvious:

(a) excessive tremors
(b) impaired judgment
(c) impaired memory
(d) disorientation
(e) visual hallucinations

However, to withdraw the person abruptly would be to create delirium tremens (D.T.s), i.e. abrupt withdrawal can precipitate hallucinations, convulsion and/or tremors. Withdrawal is best done by a medical doctor or the medical staff at a detoxification center. Counselors should establish referral units so that clients who are using excessive amounts of alcohol or those who are abusing drugs can be referred to these units without delay.

One of the major difficulties encountered in treating alcoholics is that the residual effects of alcoholism are so variable. For example, a person who drinks excessively may black out. That is, the person may go through a period of total memory loss even without becoming drunk and for no apparent reason. The loss may last for days. Then too, the long standing abuse of alcohol can lead to chronic organic brain syndrome (Korsakoff's Syndrome). The syndrome is characterized by memory impairment which causes the person to confabulate, i.e. fill in memory gaps by inventing words. Finally, although no personality constellation seems characteristic of all alcoholics, in general they appear to experience high levels of aspiration and a reduced ability to tolerate failure. In this respect, they probably appear to be somewhat dependent. Yet there are also indications that alcoholics may experience an internal locus of control

(Rotter, 1966). They seem to believe that they determine what happens to them. Ultimately, however, when personal responsibilities are too great, they use alcohol or drugs to ease the tension of their responsibilities. This incongruency between what the person does and what the person believes, creates an inner struggle which is best served by appropriate referral.

## Sources of Further Information:

Appleton, W., & Davis, J. (1980). *Practical clinical psychopharmacology.* Baltimore, MD: Williams & Williams.

Boedeker, E., & Dauber, J. (1974). *Manual of medical therapeutics* (21st ed.). Department of Medicine, Washington Univiersity School of Medicine. Boston: Little, Brown & Company.

Cleveland, M. (1981). Families and adolescent drug abuse: Structural analysis of children's role. *Family Process, 20,* 295-304.

Goodman, L. S., & Gillman, A. G. (1970). *The pharmacological basis of therapeutics* (4th ed.). New York: Macmillan.

Julien, R. (1981). *A primer of drug action.* San Francisco: W. H. Freeman & Company.

Klagsbrun, M., & Davis, D. I. (1977). Substance abuse and family interaction. *Family Process, 16,* 149-174.

Margolis, R. & Popkin, N. (1980). Marijuana: A review of medical research with implications for adolescents. *The Personnel and Guidance Journal, 59,* 7-14.

Perry, P., Alexander, B., & Liskow, B. (1981). *Psychotropic drug handbook* (3rd ed.). Cincinnati, OH: Harvey Whitney Books.

Stanton, M. D. (1981). Family treatment approaches to drug abuse problems: A review. *Family Process, 18*

# HAVE A PROBLEM?
# HERE'S WHERE TO CALL FOR ANSWERS

*ABORTION* — Abortion Information Bureau, Oreland, PA. 800-368-3336. (Weekdays, 9:00 A.M. — 9:00 P.M. Saturday, 9:00 A.M. — 4:00 P.M.)

*ACNE* — Acne Hot Line, Acne Research Institute, Newport Beach, CA. Sufferers can call this toll-free number anytime to receive help regarding this skin problem. 1-800-235-ACNE. (Weekdays, 7:00 A.M. — 5:00 P.M.)

*ALCOHLISM* — National Clearinghouse for Alcohol Information, Rockville, MD. Answers questions about alcoholism and provides free literature. 301-468-2600. (Weekdays, 8:30 A.M. — 5:30 P.M.)

*ALLERGIES* — Human Ecology Research Foundation, Dallas, TX. Provides information for people sensitive to chemicals or other environmental factors. 214-620-0620. (Monday, Wednesday, Friday, 9:00 A.M. — 4:00 P.M.)

*CAREER COUNSELING* — Catalyst, a career information center in New York City, will mail you information on career counseling centers throughout the U.S. 212-759-9700. (Monday, 9:00 A.M. — 7:30 P.M.; Tuesday-Friday, 9:00 A.M. — 5:00 P.M.)

*DRUGS* — The Food and Drug Administration's Center for Drugs and Biologics, Rockville, MD, answers queries about drugs. 301-443-1016. (Weekdays, 8:00 A.M. — 4:30 P.M.)

*EDUCATION* — Questions about loans and grants available to high school graduates for further education. Call Local College or University, Financial Aid Office.

*WOMEN'S COUNSELING* — Women in Transition, Philadelphia, PA. Advice on separation and divorce issues, domestic violence and widowhood. 215-563-9556 (24 hours).

# APPENDIX A

# Ethical Standards

American Association for Counseling and Development

(Approved by Executive Committee upon referral of the Board of Directors, January 17, 1981).

## PREAMBLE

*The Association is an educational, scientific, and professional organization whose members are dedicated to the enhancement of the worth, dignity, potential, and uniqueness of each individual and thus to the service of society.*

*The Association recognizes that the role definitions and work settings of its members include a wide variety of academic disciplines, levels of academic preparation and agency services. This diversity reflects the breadth of the Association's interest and influence. It also poses challenging complexities in efforts to set standards for the performance of members, desired requisite preparation or practice, and supporting social, legal, and ethical controls.*

*The specification of ethical standards enables the Association to clarify to present and future members and to those served by members, the nature of ethical responsibilities held in common by its members.*

*The existence of such standards serves to stimulate greater concern by members for their own professional functioning and for the conduct of fellow professionals such as counselors, guidance and student personnel workers, and others in the helping professions. As the ethical code of the Association, this document establishes principles that define the ethical behavior of Association members.*

## Section A:
## General

1. The member influences the development of the profession by continuous efforts to improve professional practices, teaching, services, and research. Professional growth is continuous throughout the member's career and is exemplified by the development of a philosophy that explains why and how a member functions in the helping relationship. Members must gather data on their effectiveness and be guided by the findings.

2. The member has a responsibility both to the individual who is served and to the institution within which the service is performed to maintain high standards of professional conduct. The member strives to maintain the highest levels of professional services offered to the individuals to be served. The member also strives to assist the agency, organization, or institution in providing the highest caliber of professional services. The acceptance of employment in an institution implies that the member is in agreement with the general policies and principles of the institution. Therefore the professional activities of the member are also in accord with the objectives of the institution. If, despite concerted efforts, the member cannot reach agreement with the employer as to acceptable standards of conduct that allow for changes in institutional policy conducive to the positive growth and development of clients, then terminating the affiliation should be seriously considered.

3. Ethical behavior among professional associates, both members and nonmembers, must be expected at all times. When information is possessed that raises doubt as to the ethical behavior of professional colleagues, whether Association members or not, the member must take action to attempt to rectify such a condition. Such action shall use the institution's channels first and then use procedures established by the state Branch, Division, or Association.

4. The member neither claims nor implies professional qualifications exceeding those possessed and is responsible for correcting any misrepresentations of these qualifications by others.

5. In establishing fees for professional counseling services, members must consider the financial status of clients and locality. In the event that the established fee structure is inappropriate for a client, assistance must be provided in finding comparable services of acceptable cost.

6. When members provide information to the public or to subordinates, peers or supervisors, they have a responsibility to ensure that the content is general, unidentified client information that is accurate, unbiased, and consists of objective, factual data.

7. With regard to the delivery of professional services, members should accept only those positions for which they are professionally qualified.

8. In the counseling relationship the counselor is aware of the intimacy of the relationship and maintains respect for the client and avoids engaging in activities that seek to meet the counselor's personal needs at the expense of that client. Through awareness of the negative impact of both racial and sexual stereotyping and discrimination, the counselor guards the individual rights and personal dignity of the client in the counseling relationship.

## Section B:
## Counseling Relationship

This section refers to practices and procedures of individual and/or group counseling relationships.

The member must recognize the need for client freedom of choice. Under those circumstances where this is not possible, the member must apprise clients of restrictions that may limit their freedom of choice.

1. The member's *primary* obligation is to respect the integrity and promote the welfare of the client(s), whether the client(s) is (are) assisted individually or in a group relationship. In a group setting, the member is also responsible for taking reasonable precautions to protect individuals from physical and/or psychological trauma resulting from interaction within the group.

2. The counseling relationship and information resulting therefrom be kept confidential, consistent with the obligations of the member as a professional person. In a group counseling setting, the counselor must set a norm of confidentiality regarding all group participants' disclosures.

3. If an individual is already in a counseling relationship with another professional person, the member does not enter into a counseling relationship without first contacting and receiving the approval of that other professional. If the member discovers that the client is in another counseling relationship after the counseling relationship begins, the member must gain the consent of the other professional or terminate the relationship, unless the client elects to terminate the other relationship.

4. When the client's condition indicates that there is clear and imminent danger to the client or others, the member must take reasonable personal action or inform responsible authorities. Consulation with other professionals must be used where possible. The assumption of responsibility for the client(s) behavior must be taken only after careful deliberation. The client must be involved in the resumption of responsibility as quickly as possible.

5. Records of the counseling relationship, including interview notes, test data, correspondence, tape recordings, and other documents, are to be considered professional information for use in counseling and they should not be considered a part of the records of the institution or agency in which the counselor is employed unless specified by state statute or regulation. Revelation to others of counseling material must occur only upon the expressed consent of the client.

6. Use of data derived from a counseling relationship for purposes of counselor training or research shall be confined to content that can be disguised to ensure full protection of the identity of the subject client.

7. The member must inform the client of the purposes, goals, techniques, rules of procedure and limitations that may affect the relationship at or before the time that the counseling relationship is entered.

8. The member must screen prospective group participants, especially when the emphasis is on self-understanding and growth through self-disclosure. The member must maintain an awareness of the group participants' compatibility throughout the life of the group.

9. The member may choose to consult with any other professionally competent

person about a client. In choosing a consultant, the member must avoid placing the consultant in a conflict of interest situation that would preclude the consultant's being a proper party to the member's efforts to help the client.

10. If the member determines an inability to be of professional assistance to the client, the member must either avoid initiating the counseling relationship or immediately terminate that relationship. In either event, the member must suggest appropriate alternatives. (The member must be knowledgeable about referral resources so that a satisfactory referral can be initiated). In the event the client declines the suggested referral, the member is not obligated to continue the relationship.

11. When the member has other relationships, particularly of an administrative, supervisory and/or evaluative nature with an individual seeking counseling services, the member must not serve as the counselor but should refer the individual to another professional. Only in instances where such an alternative is unavailable and where the individual's situation warrants counseling intervention should the member enter into and/or maintain a counseling relationship. Dual relationships with clients that might impair the member's objectivity and professional judgment (e.g., as with close friends or relatives, sexual intimacies with any client) must be avoided and/or the counseling relationship terminated through referral to another competent professional.

12. All experimental methods of treatment must be clearly indicated to prospective recipients and safety precautions are to be adhered to by the member.

13. When the member is engaged in short-term group treatment/training programs (e.g., marathons and other encounter-type or growth groups), the member ensures that there is professional assistance available during and following the group experience.

14. Should the member be engaged in a work setting that calls for any variation from the above statements, the member is obligated to consult with other professionals whenever possible to consider justifiable alternatives.

## Section C:

## Measurement and Evaluation

The primary purpose of educational and psychological testing is to provide descriptive measures that are objective and interpretable in either comparative or absolute terms. The member must recognize the need to interpret the statements that follow as applying to the whole range of appraisal techniques including test and nontest data. Test results constitute only one of a variety of pertinent sources of information for personnel, guidance, and counseling decisions.

1. The member must provide specific orientation or information to the examinee(s) prior to and following the test administration so that the results of testing may be placed in proper perspective with other relevant factors. In so doing, the member must recognize the effects of socioeconomic, ethnic and cultural factors on test scores. It is the member's professional responsibility to use additional unvalidated information carefully in modifying interpretation of the test results.

2. In selecting tests for use in a given situation or with a particular client, the member must consider carefully the specific validity, reliability, and appropriateness of the test(s). *General validity, reliability and the like may be questioned legally as well as ethically when tests are used for vocational and educational selection, placement or counseling.*

3. When making any statements to the public about tests and testing, the member must give accurate information and avoid false claims or misconceptions. Special efforts are often required to avoid unwarranted connotations of such terms as *IQ* and *grade equivalent scores.*

4. Different tests demand different levels of competence for administration, scoring, and interpretation. Members must recognize the limits of their competence and perform only those functions for which they are prepared.

5. Tests must be administered under the same conditions that were established in their standardization. When tests are not administered under standard conditions or when unusual behavior or irregularities occur during the testing session, those conditions must be noted and the results designated as invalid or of questionable validity. Unsupervised or inadequately supervised test-taking, such as the use of tests through the mails, is considered unethical. On the other hand, the use of instruments that are so designed or standardized to be self-administered and self-scored, such as interest inventories, is to be encouraged.

6. The meaningfulness of test results used in personnel, guidance, and counseling functions generally depends on the examinee's unfamiliarity with the specific items on the test. Any prior coaching or dissemination of the test materials can invalidate test results. Therefore, test security is one of the professional obligations of the member. Conditions that produce most favorable test results must be made known to the examinee.

7. The purpose of testing and the explicit use of the results must be made known to the examinee prior to testing. The counselor must ensure that instrument limitations are not exceeded and that periodic review and/or retesting are made to prevent client stereotyping.

8. The examinee's welfare and explicit prior understanding must be the criteria for determining the recipients of the test results. The member must see that

specific interpretation accompanies any release of individual or group test data. The interpretation of test data must be related to the examinee's particular concerns.

9. The member must be cautious when interpreting the results of research instruments possessing insufficient technical data. The specific purposes for the use of such instruments must be stated explicitly to examinees.

10. The member must proceed with caution when attempting to evaluate and interpret the performance of minority group members or other persons who are not represented in the norm group on which the instrument was standardized.

11. The member must guard against the appropriation, reproduction, or modifications of published tests or parts thereof without acknowledgment and permission from the previous publisher.

12. Regarding the preparation, publication and distribution of tests, reference should be made to:
   a. *Standards for Educational and Psychological Tests and Manuals*, revised edition, 1974, published by the American Psychological Association on behalf of itself, the American Educational Research Association and the National Council on Measurement in Education.
   b. The responsible use of tests: A position paper of AMEG, APGA, and NCME. *Measurement and Evaluation in Guidance,* 1972, 5, 385-388.
   c. "Responsibilities of Users of Standardized Tests," APGA, *Guidepost,* October 5, 1978, pp. 5-8.

## Section D:

## Research and Publication

1. Guidelines on research with human subjects shall be adhered to, such as:
   a. *Ethical Principles in the Conduct of Research with Human Participants,* Washington, D.C.: American Psychological Association, Inc., 1973.
   b. Code of Federal Regulations, Title 45, Subtitle A, Part 46, as currently issued.

2. In planning any research activity dealing with human subjects, the member must be aware of and responsive to all pertinent ethical principles and ensure that the research problem, design, and execution are in full compliance with them.

3. Responsibility for ethical research practice lies with the principal researcher, while others involved in the research activities share ethical obligation and full responsibility for their own actions.

4. In research with human subjects, researchers are responsible for the subjects' welfare throughout the ex-

periment and they must take all reasonable precautions to avoid causing injurious psychological, physical, or social effects on their subjects.

5. All research subjects must be informed of the purpose of the study except when withholding information or providing misinformation to them is essential to the investigation. In such research the member must be responsible for corrective action as soon as possible following completion of the research.

6. Participation in research must be voluntary. Involuntary participation is appropriate only when it can be demonstrated that participation will have no harmful effects on subjects and is essential to the investigation.

7. When reporting research results, explicit mention must be made of all variables and conditions known to the investigator that might affect the outcome of the investigation or the interpretation of the data.

8. The member must be responsible for conducting and reporting investigations in a manner that minimizes the possibility that results will be misleading.

9. The member has an obligation to make available sufficient original research data to qualified others who may wish to replicate the study.

10. When supplying data, aiding in the research of another person, reporting research results, or in making original data available, due care must be taken to disguise the identity of the subjects in the absence of specific authorization from such subjects to do otherwise.

11. When conducting and reporting research, the member must be familiar with, and give recognition to, previous work on the topic, as well as to observe all copyright laws and follow the principles of giving full credit to all to whom credit is due.

12. The member must give due credit through joint authorship, acknowledgment, footnote statements, or other appropriate means to those who have contributed significantly to the research and/or publication, in accordance with such contributions.

13. The member must communicate to other members the results of any research judged to be of professional or scientific value. Results reflecting unfavorably on institutions, programs, services, or vested interests must not be withheld for such reasons.

14. If members agree to cooperate with another individual in research and/or publication, they incur an obligation to cooperate as promised in terms of punctuality of performance and with full regard to the completeness and accuracy of the information required.

15. Ethical practice requires that authors not submit the same manuscript or one essentially similar in content, for simultaneous publication consideration

by two or more journals. In addition, manuscripts published in whole or in substantial part, in another journal or published work should not be submitted for publication without acknowledgment and permission from the previous publication.

## Section E:
## Consulting

*Consultation* refers to a voluntary relationship between a professional helper and help-needing individual, group or social unit in which the consultant is providing help to the client(s) in defining and solving a work-related problem or potential problem with a client or client system. (This definition is adapted from Kurpius, DeWayne. Consultation theory and process: An integrated model. *Personnel and Guidance Journal*, 1978, 56.

1. The member acting as consultant must have a high degree of self-awareness of his-her own values, knowledge, skills, limitations, and needs in entering a helping relationship that involves human and-or organizational change and that the focus of the relationship be on the issues to be resolved and not on the person(s) presenting the problem.

2. There must be understanding and agreement between member and client for the problem definition, change goals, and predicated consequences of interventions selected.

3. The member must be reasonably certain that she/he or the organization represented has the necessary competencies and resources for giving the kind of help that is needed now or may develop later and that appropriate referral resources are available to the consultant.

4. The consulting relationship must be one in which client adaptability and growth toward self-direction are encouraged and cultivated. The member must maintain this role consistently and not become a decision maker for the client or create a future dependency on the consultant.

5. When announcing consultant availability for services, the member conscientiously adheres to the Association's *Ethical Standards*.

6. The member must refuse a private fee or other remuneration for consultation with persons who are entitled to these services through the member's employing institution or agency. The policies of a particular agency may make explicit provisions for private practice with agency clients by members of its staff. In such instances, the clients must be apprised of other options open to them should they seek private counseling services.

## Section F:
## Private Practice

1. The member should assist the profession by facilitating the availability of counseling services in private as well as public settings.

2. In advertising services as a private practitioner, the member must advertise the services in such a manner so as to accurately inform the public as to services, expertise, profession, and techniques of counseling in a professional manner. A member who assumes an executive leadership role in the organization shall not permit his/her name to be used in professional notices during periods when not actively engaged in the private practice of counseling.

The member may list the following: highest relevant degree, type and level of certification or license, type and/or description of services, and other relevant information. Such information must not contain false, inaccurate, misleading, partial, out-of-context, or deceptive material or statements.

3. Members may join in partnership/corporation with other members and-or other professionals provided that each member of the partnership or corporation makes clear the separate specialties by name in compliance with the regulations of the locality.

4. A member has an obligation to withdraw from a counseling relationship if it is believed that employment will result in violation of the *Ethical Standards*. If the mental or physical condition of the member renders it difficult to carry out an effective professional relationship or if the member is discharged by the client because the counseling relationship is no longer productive for the client, then the member is obligated to terminate the counseling relationship.

5. A member must adhere to the regulations for private practice of the locality where the services are offered.

6. It is unethical to use one's institutional affiliation to recruit clients for one's private practice.

## Section G:
## Personnel Administration

It is recognized that most members are employed in public or quasi-public institutions. The functioning of a member within an institution must contribute to the goals of the institution and vice versa if either is to accomplish their respective goals or objectives. It is therefore essential that the member and the institution function in ways to (a) make the institution's goals explicit and public; (b) make the member's con-

tribution to institutional goals specific; and (c) foster mutual accountability for goal achievement.

To accomplish these objectives, it is recognized that the member and the employer must share responsibilities in the formulation and implementation of personnel policies.

1. Members must define and describe the parameters and levels of their professional competency.

2. Members must establish interpersonal relations and working agreements with supervisors and subordinates regarding counseling or clinical relationships, confidentiality, distinction between public and private material, maintenance, and dissemination of recorded information, work load and accountability. Working agreements in each instance must be specified and made known to those concerned.

3. Members must alert their employers to conditions that may be potentially disruptive or damaging.

4. Members must inform employers of conditions that may limit their effectiveness.

5. Members must submit regularly to professional review and evaluation.

6. Members must be responsible for inservice development of self and-or staff.

7. Members must inform their staff of goals and programs.

8. Members must provide personnel practices that guarantee and enhance the rights and welfare of each recipient of their service.

9. Members must select competent persons and assign responsibilities compatible with their skills and experiences.

## Section H:
## Preparation Standards

Members who are responsible for training others must be guided by the preparation standards of the Association and relevant Division(s). The member who functions in the capacity of trainer assumes unique ethical responsibilities that frequently go beyond that of the member who does not function in a training capacity. These ethical responsibilities are outlined as follows:

1. Members must orient students to program expectations, basic skills development, and employment prospects prior to admission to the program.

2. Members in charge of learning experiences must establish programs that integrate academic study and supervised practice.

3. Members must establish a program directed toward developing students' skills, knowledge, and self-understanding, stated whenever possible in competency or performance terms.

4. Members must identify the levels of competencies of their students in compliance with relevant Division standards. These competencies must accommodate the para-professional as well as the professional.

5. Members, through continual student evaluation and appraisal, must be aware of the personal limitations of the learner that might impede future performance. The instructor must not only assist the learner in securing remedial assistance but also screen from the program those individuals who are unable to provide competent services.

6. Members must provide a program that includes training in research commensurate with levels of role functioning. Para-professional and technician-level personnel must be trained as consumers of research. In addition, these personnel must learn how to evaluate their own and their program's effectiveness. Graduate training, especially at the doctoral level, would include preparation for original research by the member.

7. Members must make students aware of the ethical responsibilities and standards of the profession.

8. Preparatory programs must encourage students to value the ideals of service to individuals and to society. In this regard, direct financial remuneration or lack thereof must not influence the quality of service rendered. Monetary considerations must not be allowed to overshadow professional and humanitarian needs.

9. Members responsible for educational programs must be skilled as teachers and practitioners.

10. Members must present thoroughly varied theoretical positions so that students may make comparisons and have the opportunity to select a position.

11. Members must develop clear policies within their educational institutions regarding field placement and the roles of the student and the instructor in such placements.

12. Members must ensure that forms of learning focusing on self-understanding or growth are voluntary, or if required as part of the education program, are made known to prospective students prior to entering the program. When the education program offers a growth experience with an emphasis on self-disclosure or other relatively intimate or personal involvement, the member must have no administrative, supervisory, or evaluating authority regarding the participant.

13. Members must conduct an educational program in keeping with the current relevant guidelines of the Association and its Divisions.

# APPENDIX B

# Ethical Principles of Psychologists

## PREAMBLE

*Psychologists respect the dignity and worth of the individual and strive for the preservation and protection of fundamental human rights. They are committed to increasing knowledge of human behavior and of people's understanding of themselves and others and to the utilization of such knowledge for the promotion of human welfare. While pursuing these objectives, they make every effort to protect the welfare of those who seek their services and of the research participants that may be the object of study. They use their skills only for purposes consistent with these values and do not knowingly permit their misuse by others. While demanding for themselves freedom of inquiry and communication, psychologists accept the responsibility this freedom requires: competence, objectivity in the application of skills, and concern for the best interests of clients, colleagues, students, research participants, and society. In the pursuit of these ideals, psychologists subscribe to principles in the following areas: 1. Responsibility, 2. Competence, 3. Moral and Legal Standards, 4. Public Statements, 5. Confidentiality, 6. Welfare of the Consumer, 7. Professional Relationships, 8. Assessment Techniques, 9. Research With Human Participants, and 10. Care and Use of Animals.*

*Acceptance of membership in the American Psychological Association commits the member to adherence to these principles.*

*Psychologists cooperate with duly constituted committees of the American Psychological Association, in particular, the Committee on Scientific and Professional Ethics and Conduct, by responding to inquiries promptly and completely. Members also respond promptly and completely to inquiries from duly constituted state association ethics committees and professional standards review committees.*

## Principle 1
## RESPONSIBILITY

*In providing services, psychologists maintain the highest standards of their profession. They accept responsibility for the consequences of their acts and make every effort to ensure that their services are used appropriately.*

a. As scientists, psychologists accept responsibility for the selection of their research topics and the methods used in investigation, analysis, and reporting. They plan their research in ways to minimize the possibility that their findings will be misleading. They provide thorough discussion of the limitations of their data, especially where their work touches on social policy or might be construed to the detriment of persons in specific age, sex, ethnic, socioeconomic, or other social groups. In publishing reports of their work, they never suppress disconfirming data, and they acknowledge the existence of alternative hypotheses and explanations of their findings. Psychologists take credit only for work they have actually done.

b. Psychologists clarify in advance with all appropriate persons and agencies the expectations for sharing and utilizing research data. They avoid relationships that may limit their objectivity or create a conflict of interest. Interference with the milieu in which data are collected is kept to a minimum.

c. Psychologists have the responsibility to attempt to prevent distortion, misuse, or suppression of psychological findings by the institution or agency of which they are employees.

d. As members of governmental or other organizational bodies, psychologists remain accountable as individuals to the highest standards of their profession.

e. As teachers, psychologists recognize their primary obligation to help others acquire knowledge and skill. They maintain high standards of scholarship by presenting psychological information objectively, fully, and accurately.

f. As practitioners, psychologists know that they bear a heavy social responsibility because their recommendations and professional actions may alter the lives of others. They are alert to personal, social, organizational, financial, or political situations and pressures that might lead to misuse of their influence.

---

This version of the Ethical Principles of Psychologists (formerly entitled Ethical Standards of Psychologists) was adopted by the American Psychological Association's Council of Representatives on January 24, 1981. The revised Ethical Principles contain both substantive and grammatical changes in each of the nine ethical principles constituting the Ethical Standards of Psychologists previously adopted by the Council of Representatives in 1979, plus a new tenth principle entitled Care and Use of Animals. Inquiries concerning the Ethical Principles of Psychologists should be addressed to the Administrative Officer for Ethics, American Psychological Association, 1200 Seventeenth Street, N.W., Washington, D.C. 20036.

These revised Ethical Principles apply to psychologists, to students of psychology, and to others who do work of a psychological nature under the supervision of a psychologist. They are also intended for the guidance of nonmembers of the Association who are engaged in psychological research or practice.

Any complaints of unethical conduct filed after January 24, 1981, shall be governed by this 1981 revision. However, conduct (a) complained about after January 24, 1981, but which occurred prior to that date, and (b) not considered unethical under prior versions of the principles but considered unethical under the 1981 revision, shall not be deemed a violation of ethical principles. Any complaints pending as of January 24, 1981, shall be governed either by the 1979 or by the 1981 version of the Ethical Principles, at the sound discretion of the Committee on Scientific and Professional Ethics and Conduct.

Vol. 36, No. 6, 633–638

## Principle 2
## COMPETENCE

*The maintenance of high standards of competence is a responsibility shared by all psychologists in the interest of the public and the profession as a whole. Psychologists recognize the boundaries of their competence and the limitations of their techniques. They only provide services and only use techniques for which they are qualified by training and experience. In those areas in which recognized standards do not yet exist, psychologists take whatever precautions are necessary to protect the welfare of their clients. They maintain knowledge of current scientific and professional information related to the services they render.*

a. Psychologists accurately represent their competence, education, training, and experience. They claim as evidence of educational qualifications only those degrees obtained from institutions acceptable under the Bylaws and Rules of Council of the American Psychological Association.

b. As teachers, psychologists perform their duties on the basis of careful preparation so that their instruction is accurate, current, and scholarly.

c. Psychologists recognize the need for continuing education and are open to new procedures and changes in expectations and values over time.

d. Psychologists recognize differences among people, such as those that may be associated with age, sex, socioeconomic, and ethnic backgrounds. When necessary, they obtain training, experience, or counsel to assure competent service or research relating to such persons.

e. Psychologists responsible for decisions involving individuals or policies based on test results have an understanding of psychological or educational measurement, validation problems, and test research.

f. Psychologists recognize that personal problems and conflicts may interfere with professional effectiveness. Accordingly, they refrain from undertaking any activity in which their personal problems are likely to lead to inadequate performance or harm to a client, colleague, student, or research participant. If engaged in such activity when they become aware of their personal problems, they seek competent professional assistance to determine whether they should suspend, terminate, or limit the scope of their professional and/or scientific activities.

## Principle 3
## MORAL AND LEGAL STANDARDS

*Psychologists' moral and ethical standards of behavior are a personal matter to the same degree as they are for any other citizen, except as these may compromise the fulfillment of their professional responsibilities or reduce the public trust in psychology and psychologists. Regarding their own behavior, psychologists are sensi-*

tive to prevailing community standards and to the possible impact that conformity to or deviation from these standards may have upon the quality of their performance as psychologists. Psychologists are also aware of the possible impact of their public behavior upon the ability of colleagues to perform their professional duties.

a. As teachers, psychologists are aware of the fact that their personal values may affect the selection and presentation of instructional materials. When dealing with topics that may give offense, they recognize and respect the diverse attitudes that students may have toward such materials.

b. As employees or employers, psychologists do not engage in or condone practices that are inhumane or that result in illegal or unjustifiable actions. Such practices include, but are not limited to, those based on considerations of race, handicap, age, gender, sexual preference, religion, or national origin in hiring, promotion, or training.

c. In their professional roles, psychologists avoid any action that will violate or diminish the legal and civil rights of clients or of others who may be affected by their actions.

d. As practitioners and researchers, psychologists act in accord with Association standards and guidelines related to practice and to the conduct of research with human beings and animals. In the ordinary course of events, psychologists adhere to relevant governmental laws and institutional regulations. When federal, state, provincial, organizational, or institutional laws, regulations, or practices are in conflict with Association standards and guidelines, psychologists make known their commitment to Association standards and guidelines and, wherever possible, work toward a resolution of the conflict. Both practitioners and researchers are concerned with the development of such legal and quasi-legal regulations as best serve the public interest, and they work toward changing existing regulations that are not beneficial to the public interest.

## Principle 4
## PUBLIC STATEMENTS

*Public statements, announcements of services, advertising, and promotional activities of psychologists serve the purpose of helping the public make informed judgments and choices. Psychologists represent accurately and objectively their professional qualifications, affiliations, and functions, as well as those of the institutions or organizations with which they or the statements may be associated. In public statements providing psychological information or professional opinions or providing information about the availability of psychological products, publications, and services, psychologists base their statements on scientifically acceptable psycholog-*

*ical findings and techniques with full recognition of the limits and uncertainties of such evidence.*

a. When announcing or advertising professional services, psychologists may list the following information to describe the provider and services provided: name, highest relevant academic degree earned from a regionally accredited institution, date, type, and level of certification or licensure, diplomate status, APA membership status, address, telephone number, office hours, a brief listing of the type of psychological services offered, an appropriate presentation of fee information, foreign languages spoken, and policy with regard to third-party payments. Additional relevant or important consumer information may be included if not prohibited by other sections of these Ethical Principles.

b. In announcing or advertising the availability of psychological products, publications, or services, psychologists do not present their affiliation with any organization in a manner that falsely implies sponsorship or certification by that organization. In particular and for example, psychologists do not state APA membership or fellow status in a way to suggest that such status implies specialized professional competence or qualifications. Public statements include, but are not limited to, communication by means of periodical, book, list, directory, television, radio, or motion picture. They do not contain (i) a false, fraudulent, misleading, deceptive, or unfair statement; (ii) a misinterpretation of fact or a statement likely to mislead or deceive because in context it makes only a partial disclosure of relevant facts; (iii) a testimonial from a patient regarding the quality of a psychologists' services or products; (iv) a statement intended or likely to create false or unjustified expectations of favorable results; (v) a statement implying unusual, unique, or one-of-a-kind abilities; (vi) a statement intended or likely to appeal to a client's fears, anxieties, or emotions concerning the possible results of failure to obtain the offered services; (vii) a statement concerning the comparative desirability of offered services; (viii) a statement of direct solicitation of individual clients.

c. Psychologists do not compensate or give anything of value to a representative of the press, radio, television, or other communication medium in anticipation of or in return for professional publicity in a news item. A paid advertisement must be identified as such, unless it is apparent from the context that it is a paid advertisement. If communicated to the public by use of radio or television, an advertisement is prerecorded and approved for broadcast by the psychologist, and a recording of the actual transmission is retained by the psychologist.

d. Announcements or advertisements of "personal growth groups," clinics, and agencies give a clear statement of purpose and a clear description of the experiences to be provided. The education, training, and experience of the staff members are appropriately specified.

e. Psychologists associated with the development or promotion of psychological devices, books, or other products offered for commercial sale make reasonable efforts to ensure that announcements and advertisements are presented in a professional, scientifically acceptable, and factually informative manner.

f. Psychologists do not participate for personal gain in commercial announcements or advertisements recommending to the public the purchase or use of proprietary or single-source products or services when that participation is based solely upon their identification as psychologists.

g. Psychologists present the science of psychology and offer their services, products, and publications fairly and accurately, avoiding misrepresentation through sensationalism, exaggeration, or superficiality. Psychologists are guided by the primary obligation to aid the public in developing informed judgments, opinions, and choices.

h. As teachers, psychologists ensure that statements in catalogs and course outlines are accurate and not misleading, particularly in terms of subject matter to be covered, bases for evaluating progress, and the nature of course experiences. Announcements, brochures, or advertisements describing workshops, seminars, or other educational programs accurately describe the audience for which the program is intended as well as eligibility requirements, educational objectives, and nature of the materials to be covered. These announcements also accurately represent the education, training, and experience of the psychologists presenting the programs and any fees involved.

i. Public announcements or advertisements soliciting research participants in which clinical services or other professional services are offered as an inducement make clear the nature of the services as well as the costs and other obligations to be accepted by participants in the research.

j. A psychologist accepts the obligation to correct others who represent the psychologist's professional qualifications, or associations with products or services, in a manner incompatible with these guidelines.

k. Individual diagnostic and therapeutic services are provided only in the context of a professional psychological relationship. When personal advice is given by means of public lectures or demonstrations, newspaper or magazine articles, radio or television programs, mail, or similar media, the psychologist utilizes the most current relevant data and exercises the highest level of professional judgment.

l. Products that are described or presented by means of public lectures or demonstrations, newspaper or magazine articles, radio or television programs, or similar media meet the same recognized standards as exist for products used in the context of a professional relationship.

## Principle 5
## CONFIDENTIALITY

*Psychologists have a primary obligation to respect the confidentiality of information obtained from persons in the course of their work as psychologists. They reveal such information to others only with the consent of the person or the person's legal representative, except in those unusual circumstances in which not to do so would result in clear danger to the person or to others. Where appropriate, psychologists inform their clients of the legal limits of confidentiality.*

a. Information obtained in clinical or consulting relationships, or evaluative data concerning children, students, employees, and others, is discussed only for professional purposes and only with persons clearly concerned with the case. Written and oral reports present only data germane to the purposes of the evaluation, and every effort is made to avoid undue invasion of privacy.

b. Psychologists who present personal information obtained during the course of professional work in writings, lectures, or other public forums either obtain adequate prior consent to do so or adequately disguise all identifying information.

c. Psychologists make provisions for maintaining confidentiality in the storage and disposal of records.

d. When working with minors or other persons who are unable to give voluntary, informed consent, psychologists take special care to protect these persons' best interests.

### Principle 6
### WELFARE OF THE CONSUMER

*Psychologists respect the integrity and protect the welfare of the people and groups with whom they work. When conflicts of interest arise between clients and psychologists' employing institutions, psychologists clarify the nature and direction of their loyalties and responsibilities and keep all parties informed of their commitments. Psychologists fully inform consumers as to the purpose and nature of an evaluative, treatment, educational, or training procedure, and they freely acknowledge that clients, students, or participants in research have freedom of choice with regard to participation.*

a. Psychologists are continually cognizant of their own needs and of their potentially influential position vis-à-vis persons such as clients, students, and subordinates. They avoid exploiting the trust and dependency of such persons. Psychologists make every effort to avoid dual relationships that could impair their professional judgment or increase the risk of exploitation. Examples of such dual relationships include, but are not limited to, research with and treatment of employees, students, supervisees, close friends, or relatives. Sexual intimacies with clients are unethical.

b. When a psychologist agrees to provide services to a client at the request of a third party, the psychologist assumes the responsibility of clarifying the nature of the relationships to all parties concerned.

c. Where the demands of an organization require psy-

chologists to violate these Ethical Principles, psychologists clarify the nature of the conflict between the demands and these principles. They inform all parties of psychologists' ethical responsibilities and take appropriate action.

d. Psychologists make advance financial arrangements that safeguard the best interests of and are clearly understood by their clients. They neither give nor receive any remuneration for referring clients for professional services. They contribute a portion of their services to work for which they receive little or no financial return.

e. Psychologists terminate a clinical or consulting relationship when it is reasonably clear that the consumer is not benefiting from it. They offer to help the consumer locate alternative sources of assistance.

### Principle 7
### PROFESSIONAL RELATIONSHIPS

*Psychologists act with due regard for the needs, special competencies, and obligations of their colleagues in psychology and other professions. They respect the prerogatives and obligations of the institutions or organizations with which these other colleagues are associated.*

a. Psychologists understand the areas of competence of related professions. They make full use of all the professional, technical, and administrative resources that serve the best interests of consumers. The absence of formal relationships with other professional workers does not relieve psychologists of the responsibility of securing for their clients the best possible professional service, nor does it relieve them of the obligation to exercise foresight, diligence, and tact in obtaining the complementary or alternative assistance needed by clients.

b. Psychologists know and take into account the traditions and practices of other professional groups with whom they work and cooperate fully with such groups. If a person is receiving similar services from another professional, psychologists do not offer their own services directly to such a person. If a psychologist is contacted by a person who is already receiving similar services from another professional, the psychologist carefully considers that professional relationship and proceeds with caution and sensitivity to the therapeutic issues as well as the client's welfare. The psychologist discusses these issues with the client so as to minimize the risk of confusion and conflict.

c. Psychologists who employ or supervise other professionals or professionals in training accept the obligation to facilitate the further professional development of these individuals. They provide appropriate working conditions, timely evaluations, constructive consultation, and experience opportunities.

d. Psychologists do not exploit their professional relationships with clients, supervisees, students, employees, or research participants sexually or otherwise. Psychologists do not condone or engage in sexual harassment. Sexual harassment is defined as deliberate or repeated comments, gestures, or physical contacts of a sexual nature that are unwanted by the recipient.

e. In conducting research in institutions or organizations, psychologists secure appropriate authorization to conduct such research. They are aware of their obligations to future research workers and ensure that host institutions receive adequate information about the research and proper acknowledgment of their contributions.

f. Publication credit is assigned to those who have contributed to a publication in proportion to their professional contributions. Major contributions of a professional character made by several persons to a common project are recognized by joint authorship, with the individual who made the principal contribution listed first. Minor contributions of a professional character and extensive clerical or similar nonprofessional assistance may be acknowledged in footnotes or in an introductory statement. Acknowledgment through specific citations is made for unpublished as well as published material that has directly influenced the research or writing. Psychologists who compile and edit material of others for publication publish the material in the name of the originating group, if appropriate, with their own name appearing as chairperson or editor. All contributors are to be acknowledged and named.

g. When psychologists know of an ethical violation by another psychologist, and it seems appropriate, they informally attempt to resolve the issue by bringing the behavior to the attention of the psychologist. If the misconduct is of a minor nature and/or appears to be due to lack of sensitivity, knowledge, or experience, such an informal solution is usually appropriate. Such informal corrective efforts are made with sensitivity to any rights to confidentiality involved. If the violation does not seem amenable to an informal solution, or is of a more serious nature, psychologists bring it to the attention of the appropriate local, state, and/or national committee on professional ethics and conduct.

### Principle 8
### ASSESSMENT TECHNIQUES

*In the development, publication, and utilization of psychological assessment techniques, psychologists make every effort to promote the welfare and best interests of the client. They guard against the misuse of assessment results. They respect the client's right to know the results, the interpretations made, and the bases for their conclusions and recommendations. Psychologists make every effort to maintain the security of tests and other assessment techniques within limits of legal mandates. They strive to ensure the appropriate use of assessment techniques by others.*

a. In using assessment techniques, psychologists re-spect the right of clients to have full explanations of the nature and purpose of the techniques in language the clients can understand, unless an explicit exception to this right has been agreed upon in advance. When the explanations are to be provided by others, psychologists establish procedures for ensuring the adequacy of these explanations.

b. Psychologists responsible for the development and standardization of psychological tests and other assessment techniques utilize established scientific procedures and observe the relevant APA standards.

c. In reporting assessment results, psychologists indicate any reservations that exist regarding validity or reliability because of the circumstances of the assessment or the inappropriateness of the norms for the person tested. Psychologists strive to ensure that the results of assessments and their interpretations are not misused by others.

d. Psychologists recognize that assessment results may become obsolete. They make every effort to avoid and prevent the misuse of obsolete measures.

e. Psychologists offering scoring and interpretation services are able to produce appropriate evidence for the validity of the programs and procedures used in arriving at interpretations. The public offering of an automated interpretation service is considered a professional-to-professional consultation. Psychologists make every effort to avoid misuse of assessment reports.

f. Psychologists do not encourage or promote the use of psychological assessment techniques by inappropriately trained or otherwise unqualified persons through teaching, sponsorship, or supervision.

### Principle 9
### RESEARCH WITH HUMAN PARTICIPANTS

*The decision to undertake research rests upon a considered judgment by the individual psychologist about how best to contribute to psychological science and human welfare. Having made the decision to conduct research, the psychologist considers alternative directions in which research energies and resources might be invested. On the basis of this consideration, the psychologist carries out the investigation with respect and concern for the dignity and welfare of the people who participate and with cognizance of federal and state regulations and professional standards governing the conduct of research with human participants.*

a. In planning a study, the investigator has the responsibility to make a careful evaluation of its ethical acceptability. To the extent that the weighing of scientific and human values suggests a compromise of any principle, the investigator incurs a correspondingly serious obligation to seek ethical advice and to observe stringent safeguards to protect the rights of human participants.

b. Considering whether a participant in a planned

study will be a "subject at risk" or a "subject at minimal risk," according to recognized standards, is of primary ethical concern to the investigator.

c. The investigator always retains the responsibility for ensuring ethical practice in research. The investigator is also responsible for the ethical treatment of research participants by collaborators, assistants, students, and employees, all of whom, however, incur similar obligations.

d. Except in minimal-risk research, the investigator establishes a clear and fair agreement with research participants, prior to their participation, that clarifies the obligations and responsibilities of each. The investigator has the obligation to honor all promises and commitments included in that agreement. The investigator informs the participants of all aspects of the research that might reasonably be expected to influence willingness to participate and explains all other aspects of the research about which the participants inquire. Failure to make full disclosure prior to obtaining informed consent requires additional safeguards to protect the welfare and dignity of the research participants. Research with children or with participants who have impairments that would limit understanding and/or communication requires special safeguarding procedures.

e. Methodological requirements of a study may make the use of concealment or deception necessary. Before conducting such a study, the investigator has a special responsibility to (i) determine whether the use of such techniques is justified by the study's prospective scientific, educational, or applied value; (ii) determine whether alternative procedures are available that do not use concealment or deception; and (iii) ensure that the participants are provided with sufficient explanation as soon as possible.

f. The investigator respects the individual's freedom to decline to participate in or to withdraw from the research at any time. The obligation to protect this freedom requires careful thought and consideration when the investigator is in a position of authority or influence over the participant. Such positions of authority include, but are not limited to, situations in which research participation is required as part of employment or in which the participant is a student, client, or employee of the investigator.

g. The investigator protects the participant from physical and mental discomfort, harm, and danger that may arise from research procedures. If risks of such consequences exist, the investigator informs the participant of that fact. Research procedures likely to cause serious or lasting harm to a participant are not used unless the failure to use these procedures might expose the participant to risk of greater harm, or unless the research has great potential benefit and fully informed and voluntary consent is obtained from each participant. The participant should be informed of procedures for contacting the investigator within a reasonable time period following participation should stress, potential harm, or related questions or concerns arise.

h. After the data are collected, the investigator provides the participant with information about the nature of the study and attempts to remove any misconceptions that may have arisen. Where scientific or humane values justify delaying or withholding this information, the investigator incurs a special responsibility to monitor the research and to ensure that there are no damaging consequences for the participant.

i. Where research procedures result in undesirable consequences for the individual participant, the investigator has the responsibility to detect and remove or correct these consequences, including long-term effects.

j. Information obtained about a research participant during the course of an investigation is confidential unless otherwise agreed upon in advance. When the possibility exists that others may obtain access to such information, this possibility, together with the plans for protecting confidentiality, is explained to the participant as part of the procedure for obtaining informed consent.

## Principle 10
## CARE AND USE OF ANIMALS

*An investigator of animal behavior strives to advance understanding of basic behavioral principles and/or to contribute to the improvement of human health and welfare. In seeking these ends, the investigator ensures the welfare of animals and treats them humanely. Laws and regulations notwithstanding, an animal's immediate protection depends upon the scientist's own conscience.*

a. The acquisition, care, use, and disposal of all animals are in compliance with current federal, state or provincial, and local laws and regulations.

b. A psychologist trained in research methods and experienced in the care of laboratory animals closely supervises all procedures involving animals and is responsible for ensuring appropriate consideration of their comfort, health, and humane treatment.

c. Psychologists ensure that all individuals using animals under their supervision have received explicit instruction in experimental methods and in the care, maintenance, and handling of the species being used. Responsibilities and activities of individuals participating in a research project are consistent with their respective competencies.

d. Psychologists make every effort to minimize discomfort, illness, and pain of animals. A procedure subjecting animals to pain, stress, or privation is used only when an alternative procedure is unavailable and the goal is justified by its prospective scientific, educational, or applied value. Surgical procedures are performed under appropriate anesthesia; techniques to avoid infection and minimize pain are followed during and after surgery.

e. When it is appropriate that the animal's life be terminated, it is done rapidly and painlessly.

# INDEX — COURT CASES

# BIBLIOGRAPHY

Adesso, V. J., Vargas, J. M., & Siddall, J. W. (1979). Role of awareness in reducing nail-biting behavior. *Behavior Therapy, 10,* 148-154.

Alberti, R. E. (Ed.). (1977). *Assertiveness: Innovations, applications, issues.* San Luis Obispo, CA: Impact.

Alberti, R. E., & Emmons, M. L. (1978). *Your perfect right: A guide to assertiveness behavior* (3rd ed.). California: Impact.

Allen, J. E., Guruaj, V. J., & Russo, R. W. (1977). *Practical points in pediatrics.* (2nd ed.). New York: Medical Examinations Publishing.

American Association for Counseling and Development. (1981). *Ethical standards.* Alexandria, VA: Director of Press & Publications, AACD.

American Psychological Association. (1974). *Standards for educational and psychological tests.* Washington, DC: Author.

American Psychological Association. (1967). *Casebook on ethical standards of psychologists.* Washington, DC: Author.

American Psychological Association. (1981). Ethical principles of psychologists. *American Psychologist, 36,* 633-638.

Appleton, W., & Davis, J. (1980). *Practical clinical psychopharmacology.* Baltimore, MD: Williams & Williams.

Asch, S. E. (1946). Forming impressions of personality. *Journal of Abnormal and Social Psychology, 41* 258-290.

Asch, S. E. (1951). Effect of group pressure upon the modification and distortion of judgment. In H. Gruetzkow (Ed.), *Groups, leadership and man.* Pittsburg: Carnegie.

Auerback, A. (1981). Self-administered treatments of public speaking anxiety. *The Personnel and Guidance Journal, 60,* 106-109.

Azrin, N. H., & Nunn, R. G. (1973). Habit-reversal: A method of eliminating nervous habits and tics. *Behaviour Research and Theapy, 11,* 619-628.

Bandura, A. (1977). Self-efficacy. *Psychological Review, 84,* 191-215.

Barron, J., & Hayashi, J. (1980). Shyness clinic: A social development program for adolescents and young adults. *The Personnel and Guidance Journal, 59,* 58-61.

Barrow, J. C., & Prosen, S. S. (1981). A model of stress and counseling intervention. *The Personnel and Guidance Journal, 60,* 5-10.

Bayerl, J. A., & MacKenzie, T. E. (1981). Unload, don't overload: A workshop on stress in education. *The School Counselor, 29,* 54-60.

Beck, A. T. (1976). *Cognitive therapy and the emotional disorders*. New York: International Universities Press.

Berne, E. (1964). *Games people play: The psychology of human relationships*. New York: Grove.

Bersoff, D. N., & Grieger, R. M. (1971). An interview model for the psychosituational assessment of children's behavior. *American Journal of Orthopsychiatry, 41*, 483-493.

Blau, P. M. (1964). *Exchange and power in social life*. New York: Wiley.

Boedeker, E., & Dauber, J. (1974). *Manual of medical therapeutics* (21st ed.). Department of Medicine, Washington University School of Medicine. Boston: Little, Brown.

Buros, O. K. (Ed.) (1978). *The eighth mental measurements yearbook*. Lincoln: University of Nebraska, Buros Institute of Mental Measurement.

Byrne, D. (1971). *The attraction paradigm*. New York: Academic.

Cattell, R. B. (1961). *Anxiety scale questionnaire*. Champaign, IL: The Institute for Personality and Ability Testing.

Chapman, S., & Jeffrey, D. B. (1979). Processes in maintenance of weight loss with behavior therapy. *Behavior Therapy, 10*, 566-570.

Cleveland, M. (1981). Families and adolescent drug abuse: Structural analysis of children's roles. *Family Process, 20*, 295-304.

Coates, T. J., & Thorensen, C. E. (1981). Behavior and weight change in three obese adolescents. *Behavior Therapy, 12*, 363-399.

Coleman, E. (1981). Counseling adolescent males. *The Personnel and Guidance Journal, 60*, 215-218.

Corey, G., Corey, M. S., & Callanan, P. (1979). *Professional and ethical issues in counseling and psychotherapy*. Monterey, CA: Brooks/Cole.

Cormier, W. H., & Cormier, L. S. (1979). *Interviewing strategies for helpers: A guide to assessment, treatment, and evaluation*. Monterey, CA: Brooks/Cole.

Craighead, W. E., Kazdin, A. E., & Mahoney, M. J. (1976). *Behavior modification: Principles, issues, and applications*. Atlanta: Houghton Mifflin.

Crawford, R. L., Murrell, D. S., & Murrell, P. H. (1981). Confidentiality of communications between juveniles and counselors. *AMHCA Journal, 3*, 22-26.

Curran, J. P., Gilbert, F. S., & Little, L. M. (1976). A comparison between behavioral replication training and sensitivity training approaches to heterosexual dating anxiety. *Journal of Counseling Psychology, 23*, 190-196.

Curran, J. P. (1977). Skills training as an approach to the treatment of heterosexual social anxiety: A review. *Psychological Bulletin, 84*, 140-157.

Daniel, W. J. (1943). Higher order cooperative problem solving in rats. *Journal of Comparative Physiological Psychology, 35*, 297-305.

Davidson, A. (1976). Sensitization and information for nailbiting. *Behavior Therapy, 7*, 512-518.

Delparto, D. J., Aleh, E., Bambush, I., & Barclay, L. A. (1977). Treatment of fingernail biting by habit reversal. *Journal of Behavior Therapy and Experimental Psychology, 8*, 319-320.

Dember, W. N., & Warm, J. S. (1979). *Psychology of perception*. New York: Holt, Rinehart & Winston.

Denkowski, K. M., & Denkowski, G. C. (1982). Client-counselor confidentiality: An update of rationale, legal status, and implications. *The Personnel and Guidance Journal, 60*, 371-375.

Dion, K. (1972). Physical attractiveness and evaluation of children's transgressions. *Journal of Personality and Social Psychology, 24*, 207-213.

Dobbins, J. E. (1982). *How to take a test*. Princeton: Educational Testing Service.

Driscoll, R., Davis, K. E., & Lipetz, M. E. (1972). Parental interference and romatic love: The Romeo and Juliet effect. *Journal of Personality and Social Psychology, 24*, 1-10.

Dunkel, L. D., & Glaros, A. G. (1978). Comparison of self-instruction vs. stimulus control treatments for obesity. *Cognitive Therapy and Research, 2*, 75-78.

Ellis, A. (1973). *Humanistic psychotherapy: The rational-emotive approach*. New York: Julian.

Ellis, A., & Grieger, R. (1977). *Handbook of rational-emotive therapy*. New York: Springer.

Epstein, R., & Goss, C. M. (1978). A self control procedure for the maintenance of nondisruptive behavior in an elementary school child. *Behavior Therapy, 9*, 109-117.

Everstine, L., Everstine, D. S., Heymann, G. M., True, R. H., Frey, D. H., Johnson, H. G., & Seiden, R. H. (1980). Privacy and confidentiality in psychotherapy. *American Psychologist, 35*, 828-840.

Eysenck, H. J. (1959). Learning theory and behavior therapy. *Journal of Mental Science, 105*, 61-75.

Festinger, L. (1957). *A theory of cognitive dissonance*. Evanston, IL: Row, Peterson.

Flaxman, J. (1978). Quitting smoking now or later: Gradual, abrupt, immediate, and delayed quitting. *Behavior Therapy, 9*, 260-270.

Forrest, D. V. (1983). Depression: Information and intervention for school counselors. *The School Counselor, 30*, 269-279.

France, M. H. & McDowell, C. (1983). A problem-solving paradigm: A preventive approach. *The School Counselor, 30*, 223-227.

Fremouw, W. J., & Scott, M. D. (1979). Cognitive restructuring: An alternative method for the treatment of communication apprehension. *Communication Education, 28*, 129-133.

Fremouw, W. J., & Zitter, R. E. (1978). A comparison of skills training and cognitive restructuring-relaxation for the treatment of speech anxiety. *Behavior Therapy, 9*, 248-259.

Galassi, M. D., & Galassi, J. P. (1976). The effects of role playing variations on the assessment of assertive behavior. *Behavior Therapy, 7*, 343-347.

Glaser, R., & Bond, L. (Eds.). (1981). Testing: Concepts, policy, practice and research (Special issue). *American Psychologist, 36*(10).

Glass, C. R., Gottman, J. M., & Shmurak, S. H. (1976). Response-acquisition and cognitive self-statement modification approaches to dating skills training. *Journal of Counseling Psychology, 23*, 520-526.

Goldfried, M. R., & Davidson, G. C. (1976). *Clinical behavior therapy*. New York: Holt, Rinehart, & Winston.

Goodman, L. S., & Gillman, A. G. (1970). *The pharmacological basis of therapeutics* (4th ed.). New York: Macmillan.

Greiner, J. M., & Karoly, P. (1976). Effects of self-control training on study activity and academic performance: An analysis of self-monitoring, self-reward, and systematic planning components. *Journal of Counseling Psychology, 23,* 495-502.

Gutsch, K. U., & Ritenour, J. V. (1978). *Nexus psychotherapy: Between humanism and behaviorism.* Springfield, IL: Thomas.

Gutsch, K. U., Sisemore, D., & Williams, R. (1984). *Systems of psychotherapy: An empirical analysis of theoretical models.* Springfield, IL: Thomas.

Gutsch, K. U., & Alcorn, J. D. (1970). *Gudiance in action: Ideas & innovations for school counselors.* West Nyack, NY: Parker.

Hare-Mustin, R. T., Marecek, J., Kaplan, A. G., & Liss-Levinson, N. (1979). rights of clients, responsibilities of therapists. *American Psychologist, 34,* 3-16.

Harris, A. J. (1979). *Everything you ever wanted to know about good study habits (and were afraid to ask).* Unpublished manuscript, University of Southern Mississippi, University Counseling Center, Hattiesburg, MS.

Hatton, C. L., Valente, S. M., & Rink, A. (Eds). (1977). *Suicide: Assessment and intervention.* New York: Appleton-Century-Crofts.

Hefferman, T., & Richards, C. S. (1981). Self-control of study behavior: Identification and evaluation of natural methods. *Journal of Counseling Psychology, 28,* 361-364.

Hendrickson, R. M. (1982). Counselor liability: Does the risk require insurance coverage? *The Personnel and Guidance Journal, 61,* 205-207.

Hersen, M., Eisler, R. M., & Miller, P. M. (1979). *Progress in behavior modification.* New York: Academic.

Hofling, C. K., Brotzman, E., Dalrymple, S., Graves, N., & Pierce, C. M. (1966). An experimental study in nurse-physician relationships. *Journal of Nervous and Mental Disease, 143,* 171-180.

Hollis, J. W., & Donn, P. A. (1973). *Psychological report writing: Theory and practice.* Muncie, IN: Accelerated Development.

Homans, G. C. (1961). *Social behavior: Its elementary forms.* New York: Harcourt, Brace & World.

Hovland, C. I. (Ed.). (1957). *The order of presentation in persuasion.* New Haven: Yale University Press.

Hovland, C. I., Lumsdaine, A., & Sheffield, F. (1949). *Experiments on mass communication.* Princeton: Princeton Press.

Huey, W. C. (1983). Reducing adolescent agression through group assertive training. *The School Counselor, 30,* 193-203.

Humes, C. W. (1982). Counselor role and responsibilities in special education hearings. *The School Counselor, 30,* 32-36.

Jacobson, E. (1938). *Progressive relaxation.* Chicago: University of Chicago Press.

Jarvis, M. J., Raw, M., Russell, M. A. H., & Feyerabend, C. (1982). Randomised controlled trial of nicotine chewing gum. *British Medical Journal, 285,* 537-540.

Jenkins, T. N., Coleman, J. H. & Fagin, H. (1974). *How Well Do You Know Yourself?* Jacksonville, Il., The Psychologists and Educators, Incorporated.

Jepsen, D. A., Dustin, R., & Miars, R. (1982). The effects of problem-solving training on adolescents' career exploration and career decision making. *The Personnel and Guidance Journal, 61*, 149-153.

Jones, E. (1955). *The life and work of Sigmund Freud.* New York: Basic Books.

Jourard, S. M. (1968). *Disclosing man to himself.* Princeton: D. Van Nostrand.

Julien, R. (1981). *A primer of drug action.* San Francisco: W. H. Freeman.

Kingsley, R. G., & Shapiro, J. (1977). A comparison of three behavioral programs for control of obesity in children. *Behavior Therapy, 8*, 30-36.

Klagsbrun, M., & Davis, D. I. (1977). Substance abuse and family interaction. *Family Process, 16*, 149-174.

Klingman, A. (1978). Children in stress: Anticipatory guidance in the framework of the educational system. *The Personnel and Guidance Journal, 57*, 22-26.

Kluckhohn, C., & Murray, H. A (1969). Personality formation: The determinants. In L. C. Grebstein (Ed.). *Toward self-understanding.* Glenview, IL: Scott, Foresman.

Krumboltz, J. D., & Thoresen, C. E. (1976). *Counseling methods.* New York: Holt, Rinehart & Winston.

Lando, H. A. (1978). Toward a clinically effective paradigm for maintenance of nonsmoking. *Behavior Therapy, 9*, 666-668.

Leichtenstein, E. (1980). *Psychotherapy approaches and applications.* Monterey, CA: Brooks/Cole.

Leichtenstein, E., Harris, D. E., Birchler, G. R., Wahl, J. M., & Schmal, D. P. (1973). Comparison of rapid smoking, warm-smoky air, and attention placebo in the modification of smoking behavior. *Journal of Consulting and Clinical Psychology, 40*, 92-98.

Leitenberg, H. (1976). *Handbook of behavior modification and behavior therapy.* Englewood Cliffs, NJ: Prentice-Hall.

Lerman, C. A. & Baron, A., Jr. (1981). Depression management training: A structured group approach. *The Personnel and Guidance Journal, 60*, 86-88.

Lighthall, F. F. (1964). *Anxiety as related to thinking and forgetting.* Washington: National Education Association (What research says to the teacher — series #30).

Lindbloom, G. (1981). A decision-making perspective on marital counseling: Issues and implications. *The School Counselor, 28*, 208-215.

Lublin, I., & Joslyn, L. (1968, September). *Aversive conditioning of cigarette addiction.* Paper presented at the meeting of the American Psychological Association, San Francisco, CA.

Lyman, H. B. (1963). *Test scores and what they mean.* Englewood Cliffs, NJ: Prentice-Hall.

Mahoney, M. J. (1977). Personal science: A cognitive-learning therapy. In A. Ellis & R. Grieger (Eds.), *Handbook of rational-emotive therapy.* New York: Springer.

Mandel, N. M., & Shrauger, J. S. (1980). The effects of self-evaluative statements on heterosocial approach in shy and nonshy males. *Cognitive Therapy and Research, 4*, 369-381.

Margolis, R., & Popkin, N. (1980). Marijuana: A review of medical research with implications for adolescents. *The Personnel and Guidance Journal, 59*, 7-14.

McBrien, R. J. (1981). Coaching clients to manage depression. *The Personnel and Guidance Journal, 59*, 429-432.

Meichenbaum, D. (1977). *Cognitive-behavior modification*. New York: Plenum.

Melnick, J., & Stocker, R. B. (1977). An experimental analysis of the behavioral rehearsal with feedback technique in assertiveness training. *Behavior Therapy, 8*, 222-228.

Milgram, S. (1974). *Obedience to authority*. New York: Harper & Row.

Morgan, L. B. (1981). The counselor's role in suicide prevention. *The Personnel and Guidance Journal, 59*, 284-286.

Mowrer, O. H. (1972). Intergrity groups: Principles and procedures. *The Counseling Psychologists, 3*(2), 7-33.

Murphy, K. C. (1980). A cognitive-behavioral approach to client anxiety, anger, depression and guilt. *The personnel and Guidance Journal, 59*, 202-205.

O'Rear, J. M., & Hope, K. (1979). Coping with stress: Getting the message across. *The Personnel and Guidance Journal, 57*, 556-557.

Perri, M. G., Richards, C. S., & Schulfheis, K. K. (1977). Behavioral self-control and smoking reduction: A study of self-initiated attempts to reduce smoking. *Behavior Therapy, 8*, 360-365.

Perry, P., Alexander, B., & Liskow, B. (1981). *Psychotropic drug handbook* (3rd ed.). Cincinnati, OH: Harvey Whitney Books.

Rachman, S. (1976). The modification of obsessions: A new formulation. *Behaviour Research and Therapy, 14*, 437-443.

Rachman, S., & De Silva, P. (1978). Abnormal and normal obsessions. *Behaviour Research and Therapy, 16*, 233-248.

Redl, F. (1966). *When we deal with children*. New York: The Free Press.

Rimm, D. C., & Masters, J. C. (1979). *Behavior therapy*. New York: Academic.

Robyak, J. E. (1977). A revised study skills model: Do some of them practice what we teach? *The Personnel and Guidance Journal, 56*, 171-175.

Rogers, C. (1942). Electrically recorded interviews in improving psychotherapeutic techniques. *American Journal of Orthopsychiatry, 12*, 429-435.

Rosen, M., & Arsht, E. D. (1979). *Psychological approaches to family practice: A primary care manual*. Baltimore: University Park Press.

Rotter, J. B. (1966). Generalized expectancies for internal versus external control of reinforcement. *Psychological Monographs: General and Applied, 80*, 1-28.

Salzman, L. (1980). *Treatment of the obsessive personality*. New York: Jason Aronson.

Sandmeyer, L. E., Ranck, A. W., & Chiswick, N. R. (1979). A peer assertiveness-training program. *The Personnel and Guidance Journal, 57*, 304-306.

Schacter, S. (1951). Deviation, rejection, and communication. *Journal of Abnormal and Social Psychology, 46*, 190-207.

Selye, H. (1978). They all looked sick to me. *Human Nature, 1*(2), 58-63.

Sherif, M. (1937). An experimental approach to the study of attitude. *Sociometry, 1*, 90-98.

Sherif, M., & Sherif, C. W. (1956). *An outline of social psychology*. New York: Harper & Row.

Sigall, H., & Landy, D. (1973). Radiating beauty: Effects of having a physically attractive partner on person perception. *Journal of Personality and Social Psychology, 28*, 218-224.

Skinner, B. F. (1953). *Science and human behavior*. New York: Macmillian.

Small, L. (1970). *The briefer psychotherapies*. New York: Brunner/Mazel.

Sparks, D., & Ingram, M. J. (1979). Stress prevention and management: A workshop approach. *The Personnel and Guidance Journal, 58*, 197-200.

Speilberger, C. D. (1973). *State trait anxiety scale*. Palo Alto, CA: Consulting Psychologists.

Stanton, M. D. (1981). Family treatment approaches to drug abuse problems: A review. *Family Process, 18*, 251-280.

Talbutt, L. C. (1983). Libel and slander: A potential problem for the1980's. *The School Counselor, 30*, 164-168.

Talbutt, L. C. (1983). The counselor and testing: Some legal concerns. *The School Counselor, 30*, 245-250.

Thibaut, J. W., & Kelley, H. H. (1959). *The social psychology of groups*. New York: Wiley.

Trimble, R. W., & Carter, C. A. (1980). Test anxiety workshops using undergraduates as leaders. *The Personnel and Guidance Journal, 59*, 173-175.

Trotzer, J. P. (1977). *The counselor and the group: Integrating theory, training, and practice*. Monterey, CA: Brooks/Cole.

Van Hoose, W. H., & Kottler, J. A. (1977). *Ethical and legal issues in counseling and psychotherapy*. San Francisco: Jossey-Bass.

Wagner, C. A. (1981). Confidentiality and the school counselor. *The Personnel and Guidance Journal, 59*, 305-310.

Walker, H. M., Hops, H., & Fiegenhaum, E. (1976). Deviant classroom behavior as a function of social and token cost contingency. *Behavior Therapy, 7*, 76-88.

Waltster, E., Aronson, V., Abrahams, D., & Rottman, L. (1966). Importance of physical attractiveness in dating behavior. *Journal of Personality and Social Psychology, 4*, 508-516.

Ware, M. L. (1964). *Law of guidance and counseling*. Cincinnati: W. H. Anderson.

Weiss, A. R. (1977). A behavioral approach to the treatment of adolescent obesity. *Behavior Therapy, 8*, 720-726.

Wekstein, L. (1979). *Handbook of suicidology: Principles, problems and practice*. New York: Brunner/Mazel.

Wheeler, M. E., & Hess, K. W. (1976). Treatment of juvenile obesity by successive approximation control of eating. *Journal of Behavior Therapy and Expeimental Psychiatry, 7*, 235-241.

Wishner, J. (1960). Reanalysis of "impressions of personality". *Psychological Review, 67*, 96-112.

Wolpe, J. (1952). Objective psychotherapy of the neurosis. *South African Medical Journal, 26*, 825.

Wolpe, J. (1954). Reciprocal inhibition as the main basis of psychotherapeutic effects. *Archives of Neurological Psychiatry, 72*, 205.

Wolpe, J. (1958). *Psychotherapy by reciprocal inhibition*. Stanford, CA: Stanford University Press.

Wolpe, J. (1969). *The practice of behavior therapy*. New York: Pergamon.

# AUTHOR INDEX

## A

Abrahams, D., 13
Adesso, V. J., 42
Alberti, R. E., 33
Alcorn, J. D., 147
Aleh, E., 42
Alexander, B., 190
Allen, J. E., 38
Appleton, W., 190
Arsht, E. D., 38
Aronson, V., 13
Asch, S. E., 12, 17
Auerback, A., 51
Azrin, N. H., 42

## B

Bambush, I., 42
Bandura, A., 21
Barclay, L. A., 42
Baron, A., 60
Barron, J., 33
Barrow, J. C., 49
Bayerl, J. A., 49
Beck, A., T., 7, 11
Berne, E., 21
Bersoff, D. N., 38
Birchler, G. R., 47
Blau, P. M., 21
Boedeker, E., 190
Bond, L., 157
Buros, O. K., 157
Byrne, D., 13

## C

Callanan, P., 145
Carter, C. A., 56
Cattell, R. B., 29
Chapman, S., 44
Chiswick, N. R., 34

Cleveland, M., 190
Coates, T. J., 44
Coleman, E., 31
Coleman, J. H., 163
Corey, G., 145
Corey, M. S., 145
Cormier, L. S., 33, 49, 56
Cormier, W. H., 33, 49, 56
Craighead, W. E., 31
Crawford, R. L., 145
Curran, J. P., 31

## D

Daniel, W. J., 14
Dauber, J., 190
Davidson, A., 42
Davidson, G. C., 33, 36, 51, 56
Davis, D. I., 190
Davis, J., 190
Davis, K. E., 18
Delparto, D. J., 42
Dember, W. N., 22
Denkowski, G. C., 145
Denkowski, K. M., 145
De Silva, P., 62
Dion, K., 13
Dobbins, J. E., 40
Donn, P. A., 175
Driscoll, R., 18
Dunkel, L. D., 44
Dusting, R., 36

## E

Eisler, R. M., 31
Ellis, A., 11, 30, 31, 50, 51
Emmons, M. L., 33
Epstein, R., 38
Everstine, D. S., 145
Everstine, L., 145
Eysenck, H. J., 15

# SUBJECT INDEX